SHINE YOUR EYE

'Vivid, passionate and deeply insightful about the past, present and possible futures of a region that has long suffered from both the interference and neglect of the rest of the world, and is busy creating multiple problems of its own.'
— Paddy Docherty, author of *Blood and Bronze: The British Empire and the Sack of Benin*

'Peppered with chatty observations from his own travels, and with a merciless eye for hypocrisy and cruelty, Májà-Pearce goes deep into the torturous history that makes this complex region both endlessly fascinating and so hard to pacify.'
— Tim Cocks, author of *Lagos: Supernatural City*

'Few nonfiction writers can merge their own life story with West Africa's and have it all make sense quite like Adéwálé Májà-Pearce, who's made it his trademark. Simply, a compelling read.'
— Femke van Zeijl, journalist and writer

'With incisive wit, Adéwálé Májà-Pearce offers a lucid and unsparing account of the tragedies that beset West Africa, from the legacies of slavery and colonialism to the incompetence and corruption of postcolonial states. A must-read book and a model for writing on contemporary Africa.'
— Adom Getachew, author of *Worldmaking after Empire: The Rise and Fall of Self-Determination*

'A tour of West Africa by a restive writer with no illusions. His account of his overnight stay in a Togolese jail gets to the heart of his aversion to post-colonial African regimes and his empathy with their citizens.'
— Jeremy Harding, Contributing Editor, *London Review of Books*, and author of *Analogue Africa: Notes on the Anti-Colonial Imagination*

'There is a quiet rage in Adéwálé Májà-Pearce's writing. With dark humour and unflinching social criticism, he tells a personal story that intersects with the collective narrative. In doing so, he takes us to a deeper understanding of West Africa's broken trajectory.'
— Véronique Tadjo, author of the *Los Angeles Times* Book Prize–winning *In the Company of Men*

ADÉWÁLÉ MÁJÀ-PEARCE

Shine Your Eye

In Search of West Africa

HURST & COMPANY, LONDON

First published in the United Kingdom in 2026 by
C. Hurst & Co. (Publishers) Ltd.,
New Wing, Somerset House, Strand, London WC2R 1LA
Copyright © Adéwálé Májà-Pearce, 2026
All rights reserved.

The right of Adéwálé Májà-Pearce to be
identified as the author of this publication is asserted
by him in accordance with the Copyright, Designs and
Patents Act, 1988.

Distributed in the United States, Canada and Latin America by
Oxford University Press, 546 Fifth Avenue, New York, NY
10036, United States of America.

A Cataloguing-in-Publication data record for this book
is available from the British Library.

ISBN: 9781805264125

EU GPSR Authorised Representative
Easy Access System Europe Oü, 16879218
Address: Mustamäe tee 50, 10621, Tallinn, Estonia
Contact Details: gpsr.requests@easproject.com, +358 40 500 3575

www.hurstpublishers.com

To my daughter
Paris Ujunwa Ọlọ́ládé Pearce

PRINCESS

Babe of all sweetness
In so celestial a touch
You loft the verse
Onto seraphic heights
Gathering gems
Beyond the cradle.

Babe of all radiances
Harmony becomes being
Your hug of light
Coupling milk and jet
In a blaze of afflatus
Ordaining the universe anew.

Babe of all possibilities
In melody you exhale
Forged in the gorge
Of the innermost credo
By the advent of nectar
Upon the natal canvas.

Babe of all wonders
Princess of faith
The rainbow spells your name
In the hub of confluence
Melding eternal glories
And boundless communion.

Uzor Maxim Uzoatu

These imperialists have just one cliché in their heads. Afrika as an empire of slaves. That's how they see Afrika. For them, Afrika belongs to them; our land belongs to them; our subsoil belongs to them.

Capt. Ibrahim Traoré

[A] slave who cannot assume his own revolt does not deserve to be pitied.

Capt. Ibrahim Traoré

CONTENTS

PART ONE

1.	Diaspora Queen for All of Ghana	3
2.	Far from My Father	23
3.	A Culture of Silence	45
4.	The Stolen People	73
5.	The Army That Trumpets the Democratic Call	85
6.	The Most Savage Acts	103

PART TWO

7.	The Colonisation Continuation Pact	129
8.	Please, I'm Begging You	139
9.	Do or Die	161
10.	A Nation is Not Built on Indiscipline and Disorder	173
	Epilogue	195
	Notes	209

PART ONE

1

DIASPORA QUEEN FOR ALL OF GHANA

My last port of call before leaving Nigeria for a two-month tour of West Africa in late 2023 was the Seriki Faremi Williams Abass Slave Museum, named after the man who built it in the 1840s, who had himself been the domestic slave of a merchant named Abass but was later sold to another called Williams. His new owner took him to Brazil and taught the evidently clever fellow to read and write in Dutch, English, Portuguese and Spanish before sending him back home as his business partner, now a free man. Settling in Badagry in what had recently become part of the Lagos Colony of a burgeoning British empire, he built a barracoon for intended slaves pending transportation to the New World. He made a fortune and was showered with chieftaincy titles, culminating in his appointment in 1913 as Paramount Ruler of Badagry and the Western District following the formal colonisation of the country, and with it the need for native collaborators to bend the knee to the British Crown.

I was met at the entrance by a young man who turned out to be a descendant of the original enslaved Abass. The museum itself occupied just two of the forty rooms; the rest were rented out to local families, although my guide said that his long-term aim was to convert the entire compound into a 'proper' museum in collaboration with the federal government. The room I was ushered into, which contained some of the original chains and manacles that secured the inmates, measured about three square metres and apparently held forty men, women and children at any one time with just a small window near the ceiling for whatever ventilation was to be had. Mostly war captives and condemned criminals, they could be locked up for weeks on end pending the arrival of the next slave ship. In all that time, they were without facilities of any kind and fed just once a day to keep them from starving. Naturally, not a few died before they could even be transported.

In the courtyard outside, which contained the original well that was still in use all these decades later, my guide showed me the tomb of Oga (Chief) Abass, along with that of one of his reputed 138 wives. There were also two cannons nearby, each of which was then worth one hundred slaves (thirty for a gun and ten for a bottle of liquor). As I stood there, I couldn't but agree with an earlier visitor writing on her website who found it 'a bit puzzling' that he should still be honoured in this way. I asked my guide how he felt about profiteering from the suffering inflicted by his forebear, but he just looked mildly puzzled and I wasn't surprised. Africans generally have yet to acknowledge their complicity in the 426-year-long Atlantic Slave Trade (1441–1867), so much so that another contemporary slave-trading chief who built what is now the Mobee Royal Family Original Slave Relics Museum is similarly buried in his compound but with more than just his name on the tombstone, to wit (and in caps): *SWEET IS THE REMEMBRANCE OF THE JUST*. Among the artefacts on display are yokes, chains and a mouth lock, along with handcuffs specially designed for children.

When the slave ship finally arrived, the captives—up to 11,000 annually from Badagry alone by the seventeenth century—would be taken by canoe to nearby Gberefu Island, where they were marched single file to the beachfront, which took me less than ten minutes by motorcycle taxi on the sandy path. About halfway along, we passed the 'spirit well' the captives were forced to drink from because it was believed that anyone who did so would forget their past. By and by, we arrived at a beach with swaying tropical coconut trees, from where they would be loaded onto another canoe bound for the slave ship anchored in the distance. The memorial subsequently put up as part of the government's supposed intention to attract tourists said it all: *Point of No Return: Journey to Unknown Destination.*

There are many depots along the 1,500-mile Slave Coast—the name given by the European traders—between what is now Nigeria and Senegal. Badagry, which exported over one-and-a-half million in total, was the largest, but Ouidah in neighbouring Benin Republic ran it a close second, hence the concrete and bronze Door of No Return arch that was subsequently erected on the beachfront as a memorial. Less than a mile away is the Place de Chacha square, which was an open-air slave auction site with the well-preserved statue of Francisco Félix de Souza, who arrived as a twenty-year-old from the then Portuguese colony of Brazil to become one of the biggest slave merchants in recorded history. He is also the hero of *The Viceroy of Ouidah*, Bruce Chatwin's largely well-received 1980 novella which one commentator called 'probably the most unforgettable depiction of white men losing their minds when trying to deal with "Darkest Africa",' which was why the choice of Klaus Kinski to play the lead in Warner Herzog's 1987 film of the book, *Cobra Verde*, was a masterstroke. According to Herzog himself, Kinski was 'a monster and a great pestilence,' which would seem an accurate description of the fellow he played who made a fortune selling his fellow human beings over so many decades without apparently experiencing the slightest pang of remorse. 'Often on sleepless nights he would lie and listen to the groan and clank of the barracoon, only to remember the sweet singing in the chapel at Tapuitapera and roll over with his conscience clean.'

And he must have experienced many sleepless nights given that he reputedly sired sixty-three 'mulatto' sons (along with an unknown number of mulatto daughters), the descendants of whom, ironically, bestow his nickname of Chacha on their latest patriarch; and ironic because, as Chatwin tells it,

> Toward the end of his life...the slaver fell foul of his friend the king [of Ouidah], was ruined by his Brazilian partners and was abandoned by his brood of mulatto sons. He died a madman and was buried in a barrel of rum, together with a beheaded boy and girl, under his Goanese four-poster bed.

The current Chacha, a construction engineer by the name of Moise de Souza, recently apologised for his family's role in the dastardly endeavour—'It is something that makes me feel bad. We know it's painful, and all I can do is apologise'—but it seems he might be in a minority; according to Bernardine Evaristo, my Booker Prize-winning British-mother-Nigerian-father 'sister':

> Chatwin died aged forty-eight in 1989, before I could worship at his feet, but I did visit da Silva's shrine in 1992. He's buried, as he is in the novel, in the family compound in Ouidah. I was shown around by one of his beige-skinned, grey-eyed descendants, who was unashamedly proud of his slave-trader ancestor.[1]

According to Olabiyi Babalola Joseph Yai, a retired history professor, 'This is still a country divided between the families of the enslaved and the slave traders. But the elite don't want to talk about what happened here.' One descendant of the enslaved, who runs a business in the town of Ketou from where thousands were seized, summed it up: 'Our anger at the families who sold our ancestors will never go away until the end of the world.' On the plus side, Benin is one of the few which has attempted to come to terms with what happened. In 1992, it held a UNESCO-sponsored international conference that looked at where and how slaves were sold. Seven years later, the then president, Mathieu Kérékou, visited a church in Baltimore, Maryland where he fell on his knees and apologised to the African American congregation for his continent's complicity in 'the largest enforced movement of humanity ever recorded,' about twenty per cent of whom died or committed suicide in the squalid conditions they were forced to endure before or during the shipping itself.

Although Badagry and Ouidah were the two most important slave depots, lesser ones abounded. Across the border in the Togolese town of Agbodrafo (Safe Harbour) is Woold Homé. Built in 1835 by a Scottish slave trader called John Henry Wood two decades after the British had outlawed the trade, it consists of six bedrooms and a living room above a five-foot-high cellar where the slaves were crammed for weeks on end as they listened to their captors criss-crossing the floorboards above their bowed heads. It is now a UNESCO World Heritage Site as a 'monument' and 'witness' to the Holocaust that was the Atlantic Slave Trade, shaking as it did 'humanity's moral, legal and cultural foundations'. That the word 'Holocaust' isn't officially capitalised according to an international system we permit ourselves to be excluded from—the UN, for example, where Africa has 54 impotent seats out of 193 and the continent is only allowed three, non-permanent seats on the Security Council on a two-year rotating basis but without the power of veto, which is where the real power lies—is testament to the very slavery which abides with us yet, even as descendants of the latter-day Holocaust (invariably capitalised) visit the same on the Palestinian 'human animals' they were themselves once considered, such is the enduring tragedy of the human condition.

And on it goes. In Ghana, there are over thirty surviving forts, castles and former trading posts that were pressed into service. Two have since been turned into museums. In the first, Cape Coast, up to one thousand men and five hundred women were held at any one time in poorly ventilated dungeons with little space and less light for up to three months at a time. The latter were separated from the former that they might more easily be raped by their captors. There were also small, pitch-black confinement cells for the more 'rebellious' among them. This contrasted with the extravagant chambers above for the British governor and officers with scenic views of the ocean and a nearby chapel where they could cleanse their souls in the name of Jesus. It is now in the possession of the Ghana Museums and Monuments Board. Eight miles further along the coast is Elmina (also known as George's Castle) with its own Door of No Return where conditions were much the same for the thirty thousand who passed through it each year. The slightest sign of revolt was harshly dealt with: men were sent to the condemned cell, where they were left to starve; women were beaten and chained to cannon balls in the courtyard.

The slave forts in Ghana are especially popular among African Americans exploring their roots, the more so since the birth of #BlackLivesMatter, the term first coined in a 2013 Facebook post following the acquittal of George Zimmerman, a white man, who shot and killed Trayvon Martin, a seventeen-year-old unarmed black teenager exiting a shop where he had gone to buy sweets and iced tea. It seems that the youngster looked 'suspicious', which Zimmerman claimed allowed him to act in self-defence under the 'stand your ground law', i.e. that a person may use deadly force if they reasonably believe it to be necessary to defend themselves against certain violent crimes. One year later, the movement was given further impetus by the killing of Michael Brown, also unarmed, also a teenager, this time by a police officer, as was the case in the 2020 recorded killing of the forty-six-year-old George Floyd, which made the movement go viral. Ghana was especially favoured following the country's Year of Return initiative, launched in 2019 'to celebrate and build upon our shared ancestral heritage', according to the government itself four centuries after the first recorded slave ship landed in Jamestown in the then English colony of Virginia.

But then Ghana is the country of Kwame Nkrumah, the US-educated pan-Africanist who actively encouraged African American intellectuals to return 'home' when he assumed the presidency in 1957. The most prominent of them was W.E.B. Du Bois, one of the founders of the National Association for the Advancement of Colored People and author, most famously, of *The Souls of Black Folk*:

> It is a peculiar sensation, this double-consciousness, this sense of always looking at one's self through the eyes of others, of measuring one's soul by the tape of a world that looks on in amused contempt and pity. One ever feels his twoness—an American, a Negro; two souls, two thoughts, two unreconciled strivings; two warring ideals in one dark body, whose strength alone keeps it from being torn asunder.[2]

Nkrumah personally invited the then eighty-nine-year-old to participate in Ghana's independence-day celebrations, but he was unable to do so because the US government confiscated his passport on account of his supposed communist sympathies as the Cold War set in. The authorities subsequently saw the error of their pitiful response to the history they are still attempting to suppress and he was allowed to travel in 1960, the so-called Year of Africa when most Anglophone and Francophone colonies— but not Lusophone ones—received what almost everyone was pleased to call their independence. However, this was belied by the double-speak which accompanied it: On the one hand, the

UN's 1966 *Covenant on Human Rights* stated, 'All peoples and all nations shall have the right of self-determination'; on the other hand, the 1960 UN charter, *On the Granting of Independence to Colonial Countries and People*, stated that, 'Any attempt aimed at the partial or total disruption of the national unit and the territorial integrity of a country is incompatible with the purposes and principles of the charter of the United Nations.' While in the country, Nkrumah asked Du Bois to oversee an encyclopedia of the African diaspora, whereupon the country of his birth once again refused to renew his passport to travel out and he proudly became a Ghanaian citizen. He died two years later and was given a state burial. In 1985, his home in Accra was turned into the W.E.B. Du Bois Memorial Centre for Pan African Culture. It houses a small museum with part of his personal library and a collection of his works available to researchers.

The latest call to return home was seen by some as a cynical ploy by the outgoing president, Nana Akufo-Addo, to help boost what was then becoming the world's second-worst performing currency after Russia's, which was then contending with sanctions on account of its assault on Ukraine that was somehow different from Israel's on Gaza. To that end, he also pressed some US celebrities into service to help promote the initiative from afar: Oprah Winfrey, Jay-Z, Steve Harvey, Dave Chappelle, Nicki Minaj. It's not difficult to see why many would be tempted. Being part of a black-majority population is a welcome change for some African Americans, and pithily summed up by one who did make the journey: 'There is no such thing as a black woman in Ghana. I'm a woman in Ghana. We are all black,' said Lakeshia Ford, an African American interviewed in Ghana by the BBC. Exactly so, although this is tempered by the recorded response from a native to another ecstatic returnee: 'You'll still be a slave in our eyes, dog.' In fact, most of the 1,500 who took up the offer of full Ghanaian citizenship to live and work in the country were either retirees or self-employed, for obvious reasons. There are few enough steady jobs in Ghana which, in any case, are invariably badly paid, as in the rest of the subregion, where the 'masses' must shift for themselves as best they might in the absence of even the most rudimentary safety nets.

Of the two groups, the retirees with a decent pension have the best of both worlds, as indeed they have in any 'developing' country, as I know from my own experience. One thousand pounds a month from my British state pension and a modest house I own wouldn't get me very far in the UK but in Nigeria it is currently worth two million naira, or three times the salary of a bank manager. This allows both me and my partner, in her case an artist who also works from home, to employ three staff—a cleaner, an office assistant, a nanny—whose combined total monthly take-home is just £60. You get the picture: I'm all right, Jack, in English parlance. The same would hold if we were to relocate to Ghana, for instance because of a second civil war (the first not having resolved the problems that brought it about), or perhaps just the anarchy that our avaricious politicians on their hugely inflated monthly 'stipends' seem intent on fomenting.

The second group, the self-employed, already start at a disadvantage given that they are required by US law to pay taxes to the Internal Revenue Service back home or renounce their citizenship, in addition to any taxes they are expected to pay in their adopted country. They must also cope with 'underdeveloped' conditions they couldn't have foreseen, which is why many of them didn't last long, although detailed figures are difficult to come by—in keeping with the underdeveloped condition. One couple from Texas who settled permanently after moving to Ghana following the 2019 Year of Return Initiative listed the ten things that irked them in their podcast, *Expat Life Ghana: Beyond the Return*, all but one of which could apply to any of the other countries in the subregion: the slower pace of life, endemic corruption, being fleeced in the market as soon as they open their foreign mouths, incessant blackouts without prior warning, dangerous truck drivers on bad roads, poor Wi-Fi connection, and emergency services that don't work in harmony. But the worst, the one which made them feel 'a little dirty', was the 'class divide', the gap between the haves and have-nots, which is to say those with their snouts in the political trough and those without in what are unproductive economies. They gave the example, familiar enough to me, of paying the same for a night out as their cleaner's monthly salary. However, given that they opted to stay, they also listed the things they found attractive, including the everyday friendliness of people, the slower pace of life (we are allowed our contradictions), fresher food and the seemingly endless beaches the slaves were once exported from.

They also waxed lyrical about the 'constant' tropical weather, where the temperature averages between twenty-eight and thirty-four degrees centigrade all year round, which also means you can go to said beaches every day of the year if you so desire. As it happens, I am writing this in late October following my journey, which also happens to be at the tail-end of the half-yearly rains. Indeed, it is raining this very minute but it will soon pass and the sun will once more shine on my garden: bougainvillea, bird of paradise, heliconia, lace leaf, common jasmine, hibiscus, elephant ears and angel wings, along with banana and plantain trees and the avocado I planted to mark both the turn of the millennium and my claim after a long legal battle with the country's 'criminal justice system' of the property I had unexpectedly inherited from my otherwise estranged, wayward father—of whom more anon. Meanwhile, in the UK the clocks have just been turned back as the days grow colder under a waning sun, but lest I wax too lyrical there is also a dark side to the romance of the return, as is currently happening in the Ghanaian town of Asebu. It was here, in 2020, that the paramount chief, Amanfi VII, allocated free plots over an area of five thousand acres to anyone of African descent wanting to settle in the country. He named it Pan-African Village on the grounds that, 'I wanted to show our diaspora brothers and sisters that we care for them. They are from Africa and in Africa everybody is entitled to a piece of land.' He also rightly pointed out that he was giving them a reason to stay else 'they will visit the castles, weep a little, and then the next moment they are on the plane back to the US.' The only cost was an administrative fee of $1,000 per plot, payable directly to His Majesty. As of now, 560 people have taken up the offer, which means that he has pocketed over half-a-million dollars, a tidy enough sum even in the originating country.

However, according to a report—'A new home for the African diaspora in Ghana stirs tension'—the settlement 'has ignited bitter opposition in the local population,' over 150 of whom insisted that the land belonged to them.[3] One such, fifty-nine-year-old Kwesi Otu-Bensil, claimed that his family owned 123 acres they had been farming for generations—yams, coconuts, oranges—but which had now 'been destroyed'. The chief disagreed and they went to court, which issued an injunction the new owners simply ignored as they continued building. In another case, forty-four-year-old Daniel Kweku confronted workers on site and showed them the injunction but when the police arrived, his two relatives who had accompanied him were arrested and detained for three days before they were released without charge. When he attempted to go back to what he continued to insist was his ancestral land, he was told by his returnee brothers that they had guns (being American, and one from Chicago) and wouldn't hesitate to shoot him if he ever came back. Another hired a security guard armed with a pump-action rifle.

Yet another returnee, Hoyen Vivalee, otherwise known as the Diaspora Queen for All of Ghana, arrived from Atlanta, Georgia in 2022. Having recently retired, her prospects back home were bleak—'the money that I was gonna get for my social security could not pay a light bill or water rate'—but then fortuitously ran into a friend who had themselves acquired land in Ghana and invited her over to see for herself. Now she lives in a US$50,000 two-storey 'lime-green and orange' house with guest quarters she rents to visitors as she plans how to 'lift people out of poverty, in Asebu and all of Ghana,' for instance by encouraging her fellow returnees to build pay-to-use toilets. Apparently, this would not only tackle the problem of open defecation but also provide a return on investment, although it is unclear how this will lift the indigenes out of the poverty they don't seem to mind anyway; as she frames it:

> In Ghana, people are humble. They don't need much to live. Food is the most important to a lot of people. They don't even need a fork; they use their hands. They have no problems sleeping flat on the ground. I mean, it sounds like poverty, but when you think about it, how much do we really need to survive?

Which is why the aforementioned Otu-Bensil describes such like her variously as his 'brothers and sisters' and 'the whites'. As for our Diaspora Queen: 'They should have access to land but it's not our fault. We worked for our money and bought the land. Nothing was given to us for free,' which would seem to contradict the narrative proffered by His Majesty.

The other, deservedly better-known Queen is, of course, Rita Marley, widow of the legendary reggae musician. She moved to Ghana in the early 1990s—that is, before the country's call for the diaspora to return home—where, as with the others quoted above, she was just a woman no different from any other:

> Africa has come like a new life to me, with an ancient background, because it's so black; and because of this I feel at home—that fight you

face against blackness in other places does not exist here. I want the freedom to be what I am, and what I'm supposed to be, without having to fight anybody to be that.[4]

Not that she thereby lost sight of her origins: 'I see myself still as a Jamaican, but Africa is our roots and I was always looking forward to this transition. Nigeria is more like New York, but Ghana is a lot more like what we expect Africa to be.' In 2000, she was installed as a Queen Mother in Konkonuru and given the title Nana Afua Adobea, 'Nana' being a term of respect for both male and female elders.

She made the move to Ghana following the death of her husband, although she claims not to see herself as his widow: 'I still feel I'm working with him. I feel I'm still his partner,' she told *Rolling Stone* magazine in 2000,[5] hence Studio One she built in his memory, along with a nonprofit, The Rita Marley Foundation, which is 'based on the principles of love and compassion' as it 'seeks to realise [her] vision of eliminating poverty and discrimination against the disenfranchised, especially the elderly, women and children'. In 2013, she was granted honorary citizenship and in 2019 was among the first batch of 126 to be granted full citizenship. By then, she had moved permanently to Miami following a stroke three years earlier which left her wheelchair-bound, but where she is unhappy about recent developments: 'She thinks Trump doesn't like black people, and she was very nervous about what she saw happening in America with the election,' according to one of her daughters.

For Rita Marley, Ghana was 'heaven', but this was a step too far for the Texas businessman and his partner referred to earlier who nevertheless opted to stay:

> It's not the cleanest place; for the most part, there's a lack of overall 'let's keep Ghana clean'. People just throw their water [sachets] out or whatever trash there is. And there's so much plastic. I mean, you go to

the market and the market woman is going to put every single thing into a plastic bag and then tie it up and put in another plastic bag... Plastic is everywhere, it's clogging up the waterways...and rolling up on the beaches and they have beautiful beaches.

From the perspective of Lagos—but evidently not Texas—this last complaint sounds wildly off-the-mark, but then I also missed another sight that so appalled his 'brother', Ta-Nehisi Coates, the esteemed African American author of *The Message*, visiting Senegal on his first-ever African trip for his latest book:

> The flight landed, and after the rituals of deboarding and customs I found myself in the back of a car being driven into the city. What I remember with the most clarity from that first drive is a dim fear that became more legible as the highway opened into *la Corniche*, the long beach along the Atlantic. All along that beach I saw what looked like the abandoned remnants of an outdoor training gym—bench presses, a manual elliptical, pull-up bars. Time and the elements seem to have gotten the best of the equipment, and in the blur of our passing I saw yellow paint peeling from the machines to reveal the rusting metal beneath. I assumed that these pieces were the remains of some public works project gone wrong, and that the sight of this ostensible failure immediately became a sign of our collective dysfunction, of the 'Negro race's' irredeemably savage state. And hearing that voice in my mind, I came to a terrible realization: After all the work of my parents, all the *Ashanti to Zulu* and *Bringing the Rain to Kapiti Plain*, after all the drums and dance classes, after all the African names, after the entire arsenal of vindication, I was still afraid that the Niggerologists were right about us.[6]

To any visiting Nigerian, Ghanaians obviously take pride in their surroundings, as I observed on my first visit in the late 1980s, but then perhaps I have become inured to the sights which would affect the sensibilities of the average 'Westerner', as indeed I was later told was the reaction of a British film crew I took to eat *ise iwu* (goat's head, which they politely declined) beside an open gutter in a rundown suburb of Lagos one Saturday evening before heading off to Fẹlá Kútì's Shrine. To my eye, the beaches of Ghana—or even Senegal—couldn't be compared with the one I visited in Badagry at the start of this journey, which was indeed littered with those ubiquitous 'pure water' sachets relied on by eight out of ten Lagosians—10,000 tonnes daily for a population of 24 million—in the absence of clean drinking water even from the taps which still worked.

By contrast, the beaches I visited in Accra, a city of under three million, were spotless. Indeed, the only other comparable beach to Badagry I came across during my journey was in Guinea-Conakry, with just over two million people, but then neither Lagos nor Conakry are tourist destinations and therefore not worth the investment—little enough—of our self-interested politicians who invest their ill-gotten gains in saner climes (including Accra, where they have driven the price of real estate beyond the pockets of the indigenes). Consider, for instance, Ike Ekweremadu, the former long-term Nigerian senator now serving time in the UK after he was found guilty of an organ-trafficking plot, the first such case to be tried under the 2015 Modern Slavery Act. The irony was not lost on Kemi Badenoch, the London-born and Nigerian-raised UK Conservative Party leader, who attempted to downplay the role of her adopted country in the lives of her forebears by claiming that Britain's adventures in the Dark Continent didn't matter; as she said in a leaked WhatsApp message: 'They came in and just made a different bunch of winners and losers. There was never any concept of "rights", so [the] people who lost out were old elites not everyday people.'[7] It is a sorry sight to watch someone denigrate their origins—their roots—to please Massa, although it's difficult to disagree with her sorrow at 'the consequences of terrible governments that destroy lives,'[8] which is why her family fled back to the country their daughter had—mercifully—been born in. All too many Nigerians wish they could similarly flee—do indeed flee—a fact which is not answered by pouring scorn on her for telling what we tell ourselves every day.

As only to be expected, Badenoch's comments were seized upon by the self-declared enemies of 'woke' culture supposedly tarnishing Britain's glorious past, for instance Nigel Biggar, a professor at the University of Oxford, who opined that 'centuries before European colonisers arrived, Africans were enslaving other Africans, mostly by capturing them in wars and raids,' which may or may not have been the case but is hardly the point. He admitted that Britain joined this lucrative trade, eventually shipping more Africans across the Atlantic than any other European power (an estimated 3.1 million between 1640 and 1807, of whom 2.7 million survived) but stressed that Britain was also 'the first to repent' on account of 'a Christian conviction of the fundamental equality of all human races under God'. On those occasions when the British inflicted 'imperial violence on indigenous people' they only did so to 'liberate indigenous slaves from indigenous slavers.'[9]

As for Ekweremadu, it turned out that he had arranged for a twenty-one-year-old street trader to travel to the UK to have one of his kidneys harvested for Ekweremadu's daughter, an operation which would have cost him £80,000, small change for a person with his extensive property portfolio, including two houses in London, three in Florida and eight in Dubai.[10] Haba! as we say. The intended victim, who was to receive just £7,000, only realised what was about to be done to him when he was questioned by doctors at the hospital concerned that he seemed unaware of the risks involved and the subsequent lifelong care he would need. But Ekweremadu clearly had little regard for anyone but himself. After all, what was the street trader doing before but selling phone accessories from a wheelbarrow in Lagos?

And yet, in this and other areas of our national life, it is easy enough to blame our shameless politicians as if we, the 'masses'—being many by definition—lack the agency we refuse to assume. As it happened, Ekweremadu's wife, Beatrice, who was sentenced to six years in the organ harvesting case, was released while I was coming to the end of this book. She immediately flew back home to be greeted by ecstatic crowds, according to reports in the local press, of which this was typical enough:

> In Enugu State, the couple's home state, her arrival has been celebrated by supporters and well-wishers. Many see it as a step toward reuniting the Ekweremadu family, which has faced significant public and personal challenges since the case began.
>
> 'Our prayers are with the Ekweremadu family, and we hope Senator Ike will also be reunited with us soon,' a local community leader stated during a small gathering held in honour of Mrs Ekweremadu's return.[11]

Small wonder, then, that Nigerian politicians not only publicly announce the obscene salaries they pay themselves from the public purse but complain into the bargain; in the words of Orji Uzor Kalu, a current senator and former two-term state governor: 'I earn ₦14 million [£6,300] for everything in a month. With this money, I have to buy fuel, I have to travel to my constituency, I have to maintain my constituency office. The money is not enough.'[12] As regards the beach in Badagry he might have considered himself responsible for given his now federal appointment, two people sought to make whatever living they could there on the day I visited: a young man who offered me a ride on his scrawny horse, and a middle-aged woman who sold cold drinks from a cooler. What would it have cost them to clear the rubbish? They were hardly busy—my companion and I were the only visitors even though it was a weekend—but they obviously didn't see it for what it was or even much care. The same was true for the majority of Lagosians who so casually toss these sachets out of moving vehicles to clog the open drains otherwise designed to divert the tropical storms into the Atlantic Ocean of this low-lying coastal city-state. Indeed, people were heard to ask, 'Na flower I go chop?' when an enlightened governor—they exist!—embarked on a tree-planting exercise to also help mitigate the inevitable flooding.

But as I took off from Badagry to the border with the Republic of Benin a short distance away, I was also relieved to be leaving the country in respite from its seemingly unstoppable downward spiral. We had just concluded yet another round of supposedly 'democratic' elections, the seventh since the end of military rule in 1999, and I was far from alone in being close to despair at what the country had become. In that quarter-century, the population of the 'giant of Africa' had doubled to 220 million (fully half that of the subregion itself), but with a caveat. Many believe that Nigeria's actual population is closer to 160 million but boosted to ensure the numerical superiority of the north as the basis of their continued stranglehold on power from questionable censuses that only the federal government is constitutionally permitted to conduct, and which also happens to make Nigeria the only coastal state in West Africa whose population *increases* the closer you get to the desert. Lord Lugard, the country's first head of state following the 1914 amalgamation of the previously separate Southern and Northern protectorates (along with the Crown Colony of Lagos), never concealed his admiration for the northern Fulani, a widely dispersed ethnic group known for their nomadic herding lifestyle who had defeated and subjugated the majority Hausa-speaking Islamic emirates in a series of jihads launched from the Sahel in the early nineteenth century.

Under the concept of indirect rule, Lugard coopted the political structure he recognised at once from back home, i.e. a minority ruling class lording it over the great mass of peasants, which also had the advantage of reducing the number of British personnel required to govern such a large area—about two-thirds the size of the south—that yielded little in the way of revenue. Indeed, the north was a drag on the British treasury, hence the betrothal of the 'promising northern youth' with the 'southern lady of means' that accounted for much of the palm oil that drove the industrial revolution, eventually to be followed by the even more valuable crude. They have since become amalgamated (so to speak) as a single Hausa/Fulani ethnic group the better to justify their domination, although the Hausas themselves are becoming increasingly resentful at their subordinate status that becomes more glaring as the years pass.

Put it this way: Nigeria comprises thirty-six supposedly equal states of which nineteen are deemed northern, a disparity which already speaks volumes. The Fulani themselves comprise just eleven per cent of the northern population—thirteen million—and yet account for ten of the state governors. The remaining are drawn from one or other of the three hundred 'minority' ethnic groups to the exclusion of the fifty-five per cent Hausas, who continue to sink further into poverty in an unproductive economy which is beginning to unravel as I write. Indeed, it may have unravelled completely by the time you are reading this, and made more likely, not less, by our presumed new president, Bọ́lá Ahmed Tinúbú, who perfectly embodies everything that is wrong about the artificial nature of this complex colonial creation—in effect a fiction, as I have written elsewhere—of too many ethnicities, languages and religions. It defies credulity—although it makes a warped kind of sense—that nobody knows his real name, age, state of origin or even which schools he attended.

To further confound matters, his assumed surname also happens to be that of Lagos's most successful nineteenth-century slave trader—'she would rather drown the slaves [twenty in number] than sell them at a discount,' according to her biographer[13]—after whom a major downtown square is named in our continuing abasement to a debilitating inheritance we refuse to examine, history itself having been expunged from the curriculum in 2008 lest the nation's overwhelming youth majority begin to ask awkward questions. (The subject was reinstated at primary and secondary level in 2025 but we are yet to see what or whose version is to be written, although we can already guess.) What is known about him is that he forfeited $460,000 to the United States as part of a settlement related to alleged drug smuggling and money laundering (although he was never criminally charged).

2

FAR FROM MY FATHER

Although I had travelled extensively in almost all the fifteen countries of the subregion over the last three decades, this would be the first time I would traverse all of them in one go. Such a journey, covering just under three-quarters the area of the United States, would have been difficult in the early days when I only had my British passport and therefore needed visas for all but two of them, as I discovered when I was employed as Africa researcher of the London-based *Index on Censorship* magazine in the 1990s with plenty of opportunities to travel the continent. On the surface, being unable to get a visa on arrival was a mystery. I had no such problems in East and Southern Africa, where my 'Western' passport allowed me free passage because, after all, what 'Westerner' would be aiming to be an illegal immigrant in the first place? Fortunately, I subsequently acquired a Nigerian passport, courtesy of my father, and automatically qualified as a citizen of the Economic Community of West African States—ECOWAS—which ostensibly allows 'free' passage and the right to stay in any one country for up to ninety days but which you pay for anyway at the border posts, as is the way in these parts.

Government officials such as immigration are given a title, a uniform and a stipend to get them to and from the office that they might then source their salary from the people they are otherwise meant to serve. The average salary of a Nigerian immigration officer, for instance, is ₦2mn/£930 per annum, which is nowhere near enough to feed a family of four, to say nothing of rent, school fees, hospital bills, dependants, etc, hence the need for what economists call an implicit tax, and which adds up to substantially more than the official one that most self-employed Nigerians—that is, most Nigerians—understandably dodge if possible, given that their contribution will only be looted by these same government employees anyway, that being their raison d'être.

That said, in this as in so much else there is a marked difference between the Anglophone and Francophone countries (and leaving aside the two Lusophone ones: Guinea-Bissau and Cape Verde). In the former—Nigeria, Ghana, Liberia, Sierra Leone and The Gambia—the border officials are almost apologetic when asking for 'something for us' and will generally take what you give them with a smile; in the latter—Benin, Togo, Côte d'Ivoire, Guinea-Conakry, Senegal, Mali, Burkina Faso and Niger—they are nakedly aggressive, even insolent. 'Deux mille,' they often barked with a scowl, having apparently already fixed the amount by common consent, a matter of government officials who represent a severe minority of the population to begin with—just over six per cent of the population in Senegal, for instance, compared with three times that number in the US—actively working against the common good, which again is the way in these parts.

Indeed, on the trip for this book I almost got into an altercation while crossing from Senegal to The Gambia when, by now thoroughly fed up with the blatant extortion (can't you at least say please?), I threw the single denominated note on the table and snatched my passport from the startled officer's hand.

He looked about to say something but apparently thought better of it. This was not only because he perceived me as 'white' (when not métis, mixed-race, mulatto, half-caste, coloured: I contain multitudes) but also male and elderly, any one of which by itself demanded unspoken respect before I even opened my mouth, never mind all three together. The last is especially invidious given that the average age in Africa and not just ECOWAS is nineteen—the youngest demographic of any continent—but with the oldest presidents, in which seventy-year-olds like me are less than four per cent of the population. But he was also perhaps mindful of the simmering resentment of my fellow travellers queuing behind me, and which resulted in a brawl at another border post further into my journey when one young man— Nigerian, as it happened—refused point blank to pay and was slapped around before he was hurriedly hauled away lest the fifty or so passengers I was travelling with—all of them young, mostly male—decided that enough was enough. I was later told that the fellow would be locked up for three months. It then turned out that the coach operator he and the others had paid at the start of their journey in Mali—I had joined them later in Burkina Faso—had assured them that all crossing fees were included in their fare. The driver and his mate simply shrugged and told them to go and complain to their boss in the office they had left three days earlier. Worse yet, no sooner had we crossed into Togo than the vehicle broke down, and even I could see it was a serious matter as the mechanics dismantled the gear system. The few of us who could afford to do so cut our losses and continued on our way, but I should perhaps situate myself more clearly in the narrative before 'moving the nation forward'—in Nigerian parlance.

It was on this tour that I was fortunate to spend quality time in Côte d'Ivoire, courtesy of Véronique Tadjo, the writer who might be considered my Francophone sister—Ivorian father, French mother—which made me confront the nature of my legitimacy that went beyond my dual heritage, which was in some ways a distraction. We had met in the mid-1980s at London University's School of Oriental and African Studies (SOAS), where I was doing a master's degree to further my career prospects. We had kept in touch over the years, helped in no small part by her long sojourn in Lagos where her partner was the Reuters bureau chief. When I told her about my intended journey, she immediately put me in touch with Martin, one of her half-brothers, who hosted me first in the family house in Maféré, a village near the border with Ghana, and then at the main house in Abidjan, five hours' drive away.

Véronique's father, like mine, was privileged in those long-ago days to travel to the mother country to marry his white wife, whereupon he returned to his colony and assumed a high position at a time when only a severe minority of the 'natives' possessed his foreign credentials. I have written elsewhere about my own father, a Lagos Big Boy in the days when the city-state was still the capital of Nigeria but with fewer than one million people. He read medicine at Trinity College, Dublin from where he graduated in 1942, returning home to practice for the next ten years, where he was one of fewer than five hundred Nigerian-born physicians. He then won a scholarship to train as a surgeon at London's Moorfields Eye Hospital, which was where he met my mother, a trainee nurse twenty years his junior, although nursing was the last thing she wanted to do. As she told me more than once, her dream was to study beauty culture in Paris, but her parents' post-Second World War finances were not up to it, so she followed her elder sister into the only profession that actually paid you while you trained.

Admiring his moves on the dancefloor at the Christmas party, it was she who approached him when the MC announced that it was the turn of the ladies to express themselves. He lied that he had divorced his first wife, a Nigerian with whom he had two children living right there with him in the UK, and even swore an affidavit to that effect. They eloped to Gretna Green in Scotland because at eighteen she was too young to marry in England. I was born shortly thereafter. They went on to have another three children, but the disintegration of their marriage coincided with Nigeria's independence in 1960 when he discovered that, 'I am a man, I can do what I like.' This meant staying out until the early hours and then turning violent when she demanded to know where he had been, although I only ever once witnessed him hit her. It was early one Sunday afternoon. We were supposed to be preparing to go to the beach as usual, except that the atmosphere was far from usual. My father had taken a phone call in the living room but told the person on the other end to wait while he went upstairs to the master bedroom. Even then, he spoke loudly and laughed a lot as my mother, a handkerchief pressed to her face, sat on the settee close to the bookcase with the uniform collected works of Dickens and assorted medical tomes. Presently, he hung up and came casually down the stairs, then stopped, turned to her and hit her across the side of her head from behind with the phone handle, causing the other side of her head to collide with the bookcase.

As she told me later, her hearing was permanently damaged as a result, but it was also the last time he ever hit her. I didn't know it at the time, but she later told me that in her rage she took herself to the local police station, where she reported the incident. As she also told me, the nervous desk sergeant didn't know how to deal with the matter of an oyibo woman reporting her Oga husband except to call his boss, who in turn reached out to my father to ask him if it was safe for his wife to return home. The humiliation was too much, face being everything for him as for 'important' Nigerian men generally, but she herself too readily acquiesced to his continued bullying, perhaps in acknowledgment of what I came to understand as the shared narcissism that had brought them together in the first place. Instead of sitting put for the sake of her children, as some of the other oyibo wives in her position did, she fled to London for extended visits, the first time with my infant sister only, the second time with me as well, where we remained for eighteen months. Alas, she returned to find the marital bed now occupied by her Nigerian replacement, settling instead for a two-bedroom bungalow he rented for us midway to his office, and where he visited twice a week to claim his marital rights. Less than a year later, she finally upped and went with my sister for good, leaving me behind with my two younger brothers. She didn't stay and fight for her children, for which her children paid the price.

I know next to nothing about my father's first wife, whom I never met but who died in 1985 at the age of sixty-six. I once heard that she had been the favourite niece of a wealthy uncle who sent her to a Swiss finishing school in the 1930s; if so, she came to a miserable end back home in Lagos, having been forbidden any contact with her children, the elder of whom was effectively raised by my mother. Indeed, I heard one day that my father got wind that she had clandestinely visited her daughter in boarding school, whereupon he let the authorities know that on no account should she ever be allowed into the premises again. As for my elder half-brother, he was banished from our house in the upmarket suburb of Ikoyi for reasons that I never discovered, although he did suddenly appear one weekday just as we were sitting down to lunch. He started to say something about a problem he was having with his eyes but was chased away by the steward and the cook, anxious to placate their master's fury at this unwanted intrusion. As I was later told, he was raised in part by our grandfather whom we rarely visited in downtown Lagos, who rescued him from a poor relation in the village he had been banished to when he and his sister were brought back from London, and where he was required to fetch water from the well each morning before leaving for school.

He was rescued by our same grandfather, a gentle soul and retired Methodist minister of few words who was in turn banished when he challenged his wayward son for his fetish beliefs. Word had reached him that, with my mother safely back in the UK and my father's new Yorùbá wife firmly ensconced, we were visited every Sunday by a Babalawo clutching a cock, which he killed and blessed with its blood whatever it was that needed blessing, for instance the new Toyota car with a cooler in the boot for long journeys he never made. Afterwards, we were given black soap to bathe with and black powder to drink, both of which my half-sister invariably flung into the lagoon at the bottom of the front garden if she happened to be on vacation at the time. Perhaps there was nothing sinister in any of this and he had simply reverted to what he truly believed, perhaps imbibed through the deceased mother he idolised, a trader who died shortly after I was born but who had sponsored his medical studies abroad while her badly-paid, otherworldly husband wandered about the then Western Region winning souls for the White Christ of the White God used to enslave the natives.

I heard it said that it was a previous Babalawo who told his client to spurn his first-born son he had named after himself. Wanting to know more as I was about to embark on this section of the book, I sent my half-brother an email on the off chance that he would oblige me but wasn't surprised that he didn't bother to reply, just as he had earlier ignored my Facebook birthday greetings to him. On the other hand, I was also unsurprised that his—our—more combative sister did:

> [We] received the email you sent asking for information about our mother for your book. We will not be sending any information. We will not allow anyone to make money off our mother's pain. Don't

bother to reply or explain, because we won't respond. Stop and think about what it is you are requesting.

Perhaps my motives were suspicious; perhaps I was stirring the hornet's nest to get a reaction, any reaction, to break the debilitating silence that harboured decades-old hurts, and which she inadvertently—and succinctly—provided anyway, such is her investment in her own pain. As for me potentially making money out of the exercise—if only!

In fact, what really concerned me was her own mother's greater legitimacy in the scheme of things, along with the European sensibilities both my half-sister's and my own mother brought to the marriage. They imagined it was an equal exchange, a partnership to be negotiated by two responsible adults, which was a mistake my stepmother didn't make, being herself thoroughly Nigerian and understanding, above all, that not only was polygamy central to Yorùbá culture ('a fun-loving tribe of West Africa,' according to the British), but that the country itself—then as now—is masculinist to the core, the one trait that unites all Nigerians whatever their language, ethnicity or religion. It accounts, for instance, for the staggeringly low representation of women in national politics even by regional standards (just five per cent are federal lawmakers, against the ECOWAS average of fifteen), and why foreign women married to Nigerian men are automatically citizens—Naija wives, in the local parlance—but not the reverse; as one foreign man married to a Nigerian woman was told when he enquired about his rights as he faced deportation for breaking the law: 'Did you marry your wife or did your wife marry you?' Taking it to the extreme, the Igbo, one of the Big Three ethnic groups (along with the Hausa-Fulani and Yorùbá), even has a problem with daughters being included in their father's will. As one man succinctly put it: 'How can a property inherit a property?' The matter was taken all the way to the Supreme Court which, mercifully, ruled otherwise, but consider the following three recent stories taken from local media reports, none of which—alas—is exceptional.

1. Ibrahim is from a small village outside Sokoto. His 12-year-old daughter Fatima was raped by a neighbor at the local market last year. When he found out, he reported it to the local authorities and the man was arrested. There was a meeting of community leaders to discuss the case and Ibrahim says he felt pressured to settle out of court and he dropped the charges. Ibrahim says he regrets that there was no justice for his daughter but he's relieved that she's recovered from the incident and is ready to continue with her studies. 'I had to withdraw the case and to leave everything to God,' Ibrahim says. 'More than 10 times the community leaders came to me with the abuser and pushed me to drop the charges. I had to choose between peace with my neighbors or justice for my daughter.'[1]

2. My name is Ebele Onuzuluike. I am from Ndiakwu, Otolo Nnewi. My husband died September 1, 2012. Things are too tough for me. What I am passing through from my late husband's family is too much!

   They want to take over my inheritance and that of my kids but by the grace and power of God, I was given one. However, the family told me that they do not need me in the compound, that I should leave and move to the land they have given me. The sisters at times come down to fight me.

   At times, when I am back from the market in the evening, my properties have been thrown out of the house.

   As at February 1, 2021 things got so bad that the kinsmen had to step in and resolve for the family to leave the land.

   Before the February 1 issue, I lit a crossover candle on my husband's grave and was praying. The family asked what that was, I told them I was praying. One of them came back to ask why I left some refuse on the farm. I said nothing, he slapped me. The sister came and slapped me, and we started fighting. I had to call my family and they dispersed. They wanted to sell the land and I found out and started running helter-skelter. They all were aware.

They sold it and shared the money amongst themselves but they eventually gave me another piece of land. Since I don't have a house, I had to rent a place to move with my kids. I have three kids.[2]

3. I married him in 2010 and was living in bondage until October this year. Even though I caught my husband cheating on me a few years after we got married, I dare not question his movement or actions. He will even be calling the woman while with me and I dare not talk.

He may leave the house for several months, and when he comes back, I can't say anything, rather I will welcome him nicely and just act like everything is fine.

I left this October but he has been disturbing me, and I am sure he will get to me and force me back home soon...

On two different occasions, my first son attempted to kill himself and people were telling me it was spiritual. I tried to ask him what was wrong, but he did not say anything to me. I didn't know that the constant fighting between me and his father had driven him into depression.

On his 12th birthday, he wrote a letter saying that he wanted to end his life because he couldn't bear to see his mother suffer any longer.

I got the letter when I was trying to clean the house and when I called him to ask why he wrote such, he complained and expressed displeasure over our frequent fights. It was heartbreaking for me to know that my son felt this way, and it only strengthened my resolve to get out of the abusive relationship.

I knew that my children deserved better than this. They needed to feel safe and loved, and I am determined to give them that. If I am financially stable, I would just get out finally and never look back.[3]

And here, in the interests of 'balance', is a husband getting his comeuppance:

> He refused to give me the money and an argument ensued. I left him alone, and turned to dish out the rice I just cooked into a small cooler that I will take to school. Before I knew what was happening, my husband locked the door and pounced on me. He punched me, grabbed my neck, slammed my face to the floor and sat on my tummy. I thought I was going to pass out so I stretched my hand to pick up anything to hit him to get him to release his grip and stop punching me.
>
> My hand touched something metallic; it was the knife I used earlier to cut onions. I said to myself, let me just prick his shoulder so he can release me. I stabbed the shoulder a little; it worked as he released his grasp. I quickly stood up, opened the door and ran out. He ran after me from the front of the house to the back street. I kept running while crying for help until I noticed I couldn't hear his footsteps again.
>
> I looked back and saw him on the floor. I thought he was pretending, so I walked back slowly and cautiously to him. On getting closer, I noticed that he wasn't moving, I shook him thinking this must be a prank but lo and behold, my husband was dead. I ran screaming for help, calling on people around to help me take him to the hospital. When people came and checked him, he was already dead.[4]

Mercifully, the woman in question, Ọlámidé Akínbọbọ́lá, an orphan who had endured a deprived childhood, was spared the mandatory death penalty for murder after her case was taken up pro bono by a Senior Advocate of Nigeria following a public campaign. She was eventually sentenced to just four years and released in 2022, having already spent three in detention, thereby proving to the believers that—occasionally, at any rate—'the arc of the moral universe is long but it bends toward justice'.

Concerning my stepmother specifically, I attempted to have as little as possible to do with her in the five years we were forced to endure each other. I would never know, from one day to the next, whether I would be reported for some imagined slight when my father returned in the early afternoon from the government hospital he headed now that the country was independent, and his lesser qualified white boss—not even a surgeon—had returned home as apparent proof of our independence. Perhaps I had raised my eyebrows when she told me to go and clean the room I shared with my brothers or even wash the dishes my father otherwise paid the steward to do. It really didn't matter what my sin was. I would invariably receive a beating, but on one occasion—I had crudely approached the teenage house girl for sex and she had reported me—he let me know in a perfectly calm voice that he would throw me out of his house if I didn't pull my socks up. I believed him; I knew perfectly well that I didn't really matter to him because none of his children did. I also understood well enough that he was only anxious to please her so that he would be able to go and meet his current girlfriend in one of the three upmarket clubs he was a member of, as indeed he had done in the days when he was courting her—as she well knew. For him, his duty began and ended with a roof over my head, food in my belly and an expensive education.

Thankfully for both of us, he enrolled me as a boarder at the exclusive St Gregory's College—where I ate Nigerian food for the first time—and so I only had to endure my stepmother during the holidays, which could never come to an end soon enough. However, midway through what was to be my final year, I was expelled from the boarding house, having been caught yet again jumping over the wall to the protected slum of Ọbáléndé where I once caught the clap at one of the beer parlours-cum-brothels that abounded in the area. The thought of being at home full-time was unbearable so I pleaded with my mother to send me a ticket to join her and my sister. It was during the long vacation, and it happened that one of her close British friends from the old days—also married to a Nigerian—lived nearby. One morning, after my father had left for work and my stepmother was in their bedroom, I casually strolled out of the compound, but I had to loiter until late afternoon when my mother's friend returned from her teaching job. Two school chums also lived nearby so I visited them each in turn, remarking to myself how stress-free their lives seemed compared to mine, without the dread of waiting for their father to come home. Now I was surprised to discover that I simply didn't care. I was free. I was also certain that once I had appealed to my mother's friend, everything would be sorted. Of course, it didn't work out like that. As she explained over dinner after I poured out my story, she would have to let my father know where I was since he would be beside himself with worry—which I didn't believe for a moment—but promised to speak with my mother. My mother's friend was true to her word but what I had naively assumed would take just a few days to sort out took six months. This at least enabled me to write the national exams I had already been entered for, and in that relatively short time my father never again raised his hand to me. Looking back, I could see that, as with my mother before me, I had once again publicly humiliated him, although I didn't properly understand that at the time.

Véronique, for her part, had gone further than me and written an entire book, *Far from My Father*, which centres on her return 'home' to bury him although, as is the way with modern fiction writers, she hedges her bets, to wit: 'This story is true, because it is anchored in reality, sunk deep into real life. But it is false as well, because it is the product of a literary endeavour where what really matters is not so much the accuracy of the facts, but the intention behind the writing.' A number of things resonated with me, beginning with our closeted experience growing up in wealthy households as métis(se), half-caste: 'Nina realized just how little she knew about her country. She had lived in a protected bubble, from which she had ultimately escaped, of course, but only by distancing herself.' Like me, she didn't speak her father's language; like me, also, she had been forced to endure the local children singing out her and her younger sibling when they were at large, especially in the slummier areas of the city or—worse—the ancestral village: 'As soon as Nina and her sister went out for a walk, a crowd of kids would swarm behind them, singing, "Bôfoué, Bôfoué". Even with their poor knowledge of the language, they knew the kids were calling them "whites".'[5]

Again, like mine, it seems that her father ended up back with the old gods. Going through his papers, she comes across a book, *Witchcraft and How to Defend against It, a Practical Guide for Those Seeking Freedom*, and is duly disheartened:

> Nina closed the book. How sinister! She would have liked to believe that the book was there in the drawer by chance. But the dog-eared pages made it clear that it had been consulted many times. Tears welled up in her eyes. In what sort of world had her father lived? She suddenly understood that they had been separated from each other by a distance far greater than the thousands of kilometres between them.

However, unlike mine, her father remained married to his French wife, who, like my father's first, 'legitimate' wife, was just a year younger than him and a contemporary at the university where they met, although he went on to sire seven 'outside' children with five different 'local' women, by which time he mostly lived in the village where I first stayed. She, on the other hand, decided against moving back to the country of her birth and took over the house in Abidjan:

> Move back there? Her mother had certainly thought about it. But she knew she'd feel just as out of place as an African first setting foot in the streets of Paris. And then, she loved the calm flow of the days in this country she had made her own. She preferred this life to any other. The fear of having no purpose also dissuaded her. Her tomorrows

weren't her own in that city. Life went on without her. When she was in France, she felt like an intruder. So, when all was said and done, she stuck with the choice she'd made. And it was that choice—her stubbornness—that her parents had likely never understood. They had often thought she'd made a mistake.

But then, unlike my mother, she was an artist, someone with a vocation who could take inspiration directly from her adopted culture and blend with her own. As an old friend of hers tells her daughter:

> I take the chance of sending you this message like one might throw a message in a bottle into the sea. I used to live in Côte d'Ivoire, in Abidjan, where I was the director of a school of music and dance, 'Arts en Mouvement,' located in the Plateau, near the Abidjan–Niger Railroad Station. I knew your parents quite well, especially your mother, with whom I often spoke about her musical compositions—especially her experimental phase, when she wrote compositions blending African and Western rhythms.

My own mother, by contrast, was a housewife with nothing much to do outside of being married to a wealthy man, having escaped the drudgery of bombed-out post-war London where everything was rationed. She once told me how she had been enchanted by Somerset Maugham's novels (she was a voracious reader) set in another British-acquired tropical paradise and fantasised about sleeping under a mosquito net, although she hadn't imagined the brightly-coloured array of tropical fruits—avocado, banana, mango, melon, orange, pineapple—on sale for British pennies that assailed her the moment she stepped off the ship in late February after a two-week voyage from the tail-end of a Liverpool winter via the Canary Islands and Freetown. In other words, she hadn't the slightest interest in the culture she had married into, only the benefits to be gained from it, just as her husband merely desired the status afforded by a pretty, young white woman at a time when the white man was still directly in charge everywhere you turned.

Their marriage was a fantasy forged in the rigs of the times, which was why it crumbled so quickly; and while it is true that my father never introduced her—or his children—to any aspect of his culture (he only ever spoke Yorùbá when on the phone with a relative or friend) because he didn't believe in its intrinsic worth, it is also the case that in this he was hardly unusual. My mother, on the other hand, might at least have tried acquainting herself with her husband's traditional cuisine, like Véronique's mother, for instance, who 'took to this new diet happily' but balanced it out by eating 'a tremendous amount of fruit'. Instead of which, we would sit at one end of the dining table at breakfast eating bacon and eggs while he supped ogi with akara at the other, all the while grinning in self-congratulation at the oyibo children he sent to St Saviour's Primary School that served the expatriate civil servants who were our neighbours on either side, complete with teachers from the motherland. My mother's main hobby was sewing clothes for herself and her tight circle of European women married to Nigerian men, most of whose marriages also ended in disaster. At one point, he rented her a shop in downtown Lagos where she sold Italian shoes and handbags, but it was obviously a hobby and didn't last long. Otherwise, every Tuesday morning she took herself off to Kingsway department store in her green and white two-door Metropolitan car for the weekly shopping. And every Sunday (the rains permitting), she took us off to Bar Beach, where she would lie under the sun as we waded into the warm Atlantic Ocean with the strong undercurrent that killed the child of an uncle married to a West Indian.

West Indian women married to African men feature in V.S. Naipaul's much-opinionated essay 'The Crocodiles of Yamoussoukro', which is set in Côte d'Ivoire and abounds in the sweeping generalisations he otherwise claimed to abhor, à la

Joseph Conrad, one of his—and my—early influences (and, no, *Heart of Darkness* is not 'racist', quite the contrary in fact), to wit: 'My task, which I am trying to achieve is, by the power of the written word, to make you hear, to make you feel—it is, before all, to make you see.'

On the one side is Arlette from Martinique, who disapproves of the attitude of her fellow West Indian sisters:

> Arlette said that in the Ivory Coast the French West Indians, les antillais, behaved like French people. They looked down on the Africans and—because they thought of themselves as civilized and French—they expected the Africans to look up to them. 'Mais il sont déçus.' The West Indians made an error; Africans looked up to nobody; and life was as a result full of stress for some West Indians in the Ivory Coast.[6]

She was also of the view that 'Africans believed in independent relationships' and 'didn't look for or expect sexual fidelity'. To imagine it a reason for divorce 'would be considered frivolous': 'In a marriage the most important relationship was...between families. And that was why West Indian women...who married Ivorian men found themselves in trouble... The men simply said goodbye.' It was for this reason that Andrée from Guadeloupe, who met her husband in Paris and whose marriage broke up four years after they relocated, was of the view that 'Françaises, French women like herself, should stay in France... In the Ivory Coast the Ivorian families broke the marriages up.'

As Naipaul opined, 'It was easier for a white woman to marry an African... The white woman would know she was marrying exotically; that would be part of the attraction. The West Indian woman, with her own racial ideas, would be looking in Africa for a double security.' He also thought that 'West Indian women, whatever their background, were house proud; they found Africans dirty.' Like Ghana's Diaspora Queen for All come to save the natives from themselves while saving herself from poverty back home even as she praised the Ghanaians for being so grateful for so little, one is almost tempted to sing hallelujah for the slavery that transported her and Naipaul's West Indian sisters to the New World.

As it happened, Véronique's mother preceded her husband and was buried in the cemetery in Maféré, which Véronique asked Martin to show me. It was strange because there were four plots for the nuclear family but nothing for those born out of wedlock, although Martin himself, a soft-spoken, mild-mannered man I quickly warmed to, just shrugged and smiled when I said something to that effect. Véronique later told me that her full sibling, who lived in Japan, was 'bitter' at their father, 'doesn't understand the place and doesn't want to understand the place'. He even refused to return to the country to bury him, unlike Véronique, who still loved her father despite the 'betrayal' of his 'official' family.

I envied Véronique. She was grounded in a way denied me. It wasn't only that my mother was herself an interloper but that my father proved categorically that he cared nothing for me after I left. He did, once, write me from his upmarket flat behind Harrods in London, but not to invite me over, just to let me know he was in town. I had just finished my first year at university paid for by the British taxpayer and wrote back to tell him I was broke, only to receive a curt reply to the effect that I shouldn't bother him for money, along with a cheque for ten pounds, which I promptly tore in half—I have always been impetuous—and sent right back to him. Two years later, he was in London again and sent me a message that he wanted to meet up. By then, both my brothers were in town and staying with our mother and sister, who had been filled with stories over the years about what a horrible person he was. My mother talked him into treating us all to a night out at Ronnie Scott's, the famous jazz club where Elvin Jones, the drummer who had played with Miles

Davis, was headlining and where she insisted on ordering the most expensive wine, my father wincing each time but putting on a brave face. Later, he followed us back to the house, where they slept together on a makeshift bed in the living room of the pokey, two-bedroom flat in downmarket Ealing; and I remember how awkward my brothers and I felt huddled around the narrow kitchen table with our father the next morning (our sister and mother refused to leave their respective rooms except to use the bathroom) before he set off to his other wife waiting in the flat behind Harrods. Shortly afterwards, our sixteen-year-old sister ran away, first to France, then Germany, never to return. Some years later, as my mother neared her own death and was lamenting that her daughter had cut her off completely, I asked her why on earth she had slept with him that night. 'I thought we could be a family again,' she replied, but had the good grace to blush and turn away.

The last time I saw my father was on a spring day in 1981 just months before he died at the age of sixty-five, six years younger than I am as I write these words. It was obvious even then that he wasn't long for this world, and true enough he didn't last the year although I only got to know through my mother, who herself heard through another old British friend married to a Nigerian and still living in Lagos. When I returned to the country two years later—and fourteen after I had originally left—I visited his grave and noticed there was only one other spot, which was reserved for my stepmother.

Véronique's father, by contrast, remained faithful to her mother despite his outside peccadilloes; and yet I want to believe that both our fathers shared more in common than they did with most of their 'village' compatriots, beginning with the open levels of racism they experienced in the course of their betterment in the colonial heartland, and inconceivable today. In my father's case, it was the purported 'No Irish, No Blacks, No

Dogs' signs at rental properties or, as my mother recounted, the apoplectic London bus conductor shouting at his 'wog' customer to fuck off back to the African bush and take his 'nigger-loving white whore' with him before throwing his change at him. Back at home, my father wouldn't even have been on a public bus in the first place, let alone insulted by someone whose salary he paid just as he paid the myriad servants he employed to serve him. It was no coincidence that my parents' marriage started to disintegrate once the artificial creation of a foreign conquering power was granted a flag, a national anthem and an impotent seat on the United Nations which he mistook for independence, with his, 'I'm a man, I can do what I like,' before beating the woman who was to pay the price for all the insults he had been forced to endure because he was black, African, inferior. Véronique's father was merely a gentler version; as he said to his own wife in exasperation: 'You don't get it. There are too many things that you just can't understand. With your Western ideas, you think you're smarter than everyone else, but you really don't know anything at all. I'm starting to get fed up with your criticism!'

Since their deaths, Véronique has single-handedly kept both of the family establishments up and running (both were staffed by full-time servants, which was why it was easy enough to stay in them), but was perhaps sceptical—like the novel's protagonist—about living in the country, as she reveals when questioned by a former lover she runs into:

> 'If you are so sad at the thought of leaving, why don't you just move back here for good?' His question upset her. 'Move back for whom? For you? To give us another chance?' He didn't answer right away. 'No, for yourself.' She noted that he wasn't committing himself. He continued, 'You need a change. Now's the time to come back and settle down.' 'But why would I make such a decision?' she shot back, trying to goad him, more than anything else. 'That wouldn't make any sense. It's just

chaos here.' 'Look around you. What do you see? People getting up early and heading off to work, raising their kids the best they can, and standing up to the challenge of daily life. Despite everything going on around them. It's thanks to them that this country is still on its feet.' 'But, no... don't you see? I'm less optimistic than you are. War can break out again at any moment. Many other countries have a lot more to offer. Why should I waste my life here?' 'Really, Nina, I don't know what to tell you... That's a question only you can answer.'

For me, it was the exact opposite. The moment I understood that I wanted to be an author and not a history professor, I found myself writing only about Nigeria and hankering to be back there precisely because I knew so little about it. Fortunately (and much to my surprise), my father had left me a small property in Surulere, a solidly middle-class suburb of Lagos from where I am writing these lines, having settled in it thirty years ago. In other words, he was much more useful to me dead than alive, a melancholy fact but true, nonetheless, which could also be said in a wider sense of Côte d'Ivoire's president, Alassane Ouattara, the eighty-year-old 'father of the nation' whose decision to tamper with the constitution to give himself a third term almost plunged the country into chaos, of which more anon.

3

A CULTURE OF SILENCE

I first journeyed in the subregion in late 1989 when I was engaged by an American foundation to write a report on the press in four of the English-speaking countries—Nigeria needed its own given its sheer size—to be published as a supplement in *Index on Censorship*, where I had recently been appointed Africa researcher, doubtless helped by my recently acquired masters from SOAS. It was the first anniversary of the fall of the Berlin Wall and with it the end of the Cold War that had itself given birth to the magazine in 1972, initially to publish banned literature from the then Soviet Union but which gradually expanded its remit to include human rights abuses the world over; but what I didn't grasp in that far-off, pre-internet age with only fixed phone lines (themselves scarce in the continent), was that Africa was now considered the soft underbelly of a hitherto polarised world. 'Western' foundations awash with money were happy to pay me to write lengthy articles on the embattled independent press, along with the lawyers who defended them and the university lecturers who published in them—there was no such thing as independent radio or TV, which we also lobbied for—that was supposedly critical to the triumph of 'Western' democracy that would eventually conquer the globe (end of history and all that) with the demise of the one-party states (whether in or out of uniform) which had previously been encouraged for the sake of the 'stability' that was a euphemism for continued foreign, i.e. 'Western', control.

Take Ghana's Kwame Nkrumah, who argued for 'a Union or Commonwealth of African States' that would 'achieve the complete liquidation of imperialism, colonialism and neocolonialism in Africa' that was against the UN's own 'freedom charter'.[1] To realise this noble goal, which is even more imperative now in our ever more globalised world, a free press was considered central: 'The African press has a vital role to play in the revolution which is now sweeping our continent... It must explain the necessity for, and meaning of, the union government of Africa.'[2] To that end, he founded the Ghana News Agency to correct the distortions about the continent in the foreign media, followed by the Ghana Institute of Journalism as a training centre for African journalists. But neither the time nor the man was up to the challenge, and he eventually fell prey to the seductions of power. In 1963, he enacted the first Newspaper Licensing Law; the following year, he transmuted into executive president of 'a socialist single-party state'. He was overthrown three years later, apparently in connivance with the CIA according to recently declassified US documents—so what's new?—in the first of the many military coups that were to plague the subregion over the next three decades.

By the time of my first visit, the still youthful and charismatic Flt. Lt. Jerry John Rawlings was very much in charge. The son of a Scottish father and Ghanaian mother (my 'brother' in reverse, you might say), he first came to power in 1979 when he overthrew the last of the hopelessly inept military juntas that followed Nkrumah's ousting. He was in office for just 112 days before he handed over to a civilian government that he himself overthrew two years later, whereupon he was to remain in power until 2001, the last eight as a civilian president. He was generally well liked, even criticising the 'culture of silence [that] must not be permitted to return' because otherwise 'freedom and justice will elude us'. He also castigated journalists for 'the apathy, timidity, fear, lack of concern, self-centredness or whatever it may be which prevents too many of us from speaking out boldly,' and called for 'an independent paper of real substance'.[3]

Such plain speaking, rare enough at the time, earned him the moniker 'Junior Jesus' but the reality was the opposite, as I discovered when I spent time with Kabral Blay-Amihere. I had met Kabral in the UK in 1988, the year before I travelled in the subregion. He had come to do a short course at the London School of Economics as a respite from the challenges of 'speaking out boldly'. This followed the closure of the *Free Press*, the newspaper he cofounded precisely to take advantage of the supposed newfound freedom and 'play a watchdog role in society'. As he wrote at the time:

> What has kept us going is a realization that what we write is but an echo of secret murmuring and complaints of the wider society. But in a society where everyone feels so emasculated as to only complain in the secrecy of their bedrooms, a time comes when lonely voices feel the compulsion to behave like all the others.[4]

Indeed, Kabral's predecessor in the editor's chair, John Kugblenu, died a few weeks after he was released from detention for his criticism of the regime, presumably from wounds inflicted under interrogation at the notorious Nsawam Medium Security Prison. He was just forty-nine. According to Mike Adjei, a colleague who shared a cell with him, it was a mark of the times that the Ghana Association of Writers, 'which a few months earlier had sent a protest letter to President P. W. Botha of South

Africa demanding the release of Nelson Mandela,' failed to send a delegation to the funeral. Worse yet, the Ghana Journalists Association 'sent neither a delegation nor a wreath,' although English PEN 'sent Christmas cards to us.'

As a former director of the Institute of Journalism, Blay-Amihere was obviously well known within newspaper circles. When I arrived at his Accra office, a bare room with two wooden tables and an assortment of broken-down chairs, he was putting the finishing touches to the sports paper he now edited with Kweku Baako, his deputy. In the prevailing 'culture of silence,' these four-page weeklies were the only outlet for the country's self-respecting journalists. I counted fifteen of them; someone told me there were at least twenty. By all accounts, Ghanaians are football-mad but for a country with a population of only twelve million at the time—it has since more than doubled to thirty-two million, in keeping with the exploding demographics of Africa as a whole—this number seemed excessive.

Later, over lunch at an open-air restaurant following my meeting with Kabral, Baako, the former research assistant with the *Free Press*, alluded to his own experience in detention. He was a soft-spoken man, and I had to lean forward to hear him properly:

> Altogether, I was inside for more than a year without charge or trial. They kept coming day and night. Different people. By the end of the second week, I was lying on the floor of my cell covered in my own shit and piss. A doctor came. He said: 'If this man doesn't receive immediate medical attention, he will be dead within a week.'
>
> That doctor saved my life. If not for him, I wouldn't be here today. Afterwards, it wasn't so bad except they wouldn't allow anybody to visit me, not even my family. My mother was looking for me everywhere. She didn't know where I was, or even if I was still alive.

A CULTURE OF SILENCE

At that moment, as if on cue, a soldier entered. Baako fell silent and watched him cross the courtyard. I thought at first that he was understandably fearful of being overheard, part of that culture of silence which made people instinctively lower their voices and glance over their shoulders whenever the topic became politically sensitive; but I was soon to understand, as I got to know him better, that someone who has been so close to death can no longer be easily intimidated. In a sense, the worst had been done to him. And when the soldier, a major, disappeared into an adjoining room, he leaned forward and said: 'That was my first interrogator. He knows me but he won't look at me. We grew up together in this very district, about two streets away. I see him from time to time, but he never looks at me.'

The major re-emerged a few minutes later and walked briskly back the way he had come, his dark glasses giving nothing away. Baako, as before, watched him come to within a foot of our table. It wasn't possible to read his expression, and my imagination couldn't encompass the conflicting emotions that must have been stirred up by so unwelcome a sight. Perhaps his silence was his only weapon; perhaps it was the only kind of revenge possible, always assuming that revenge is among the human possibilities. I don't know. I only know that I felt an impersonal hatred for the uniformed thug and not merely because I had been drawn to Baako from the first, by what I recognised as an unusual kind of courage and integrity.

Later that same day, Kabral took me round to see the staff of the government-owned and supposedly largest-circulation newspaper, the *Daily Graphic*. The figure of one-hundred-and-fifty thousand in daily sales was quoted by everyone I met. Later, as we walked back to the car, we were confronted by a telling sight: all over the courtyard of the extensive premises, and all along the outside wall between the building and the main road, great piles of unsold newspapers dating back a month were being bought in job-lots by women traders who would use them to wrap the food they sold in the market. Considering the contents of the paper, it was perhaps a fitting end to what can only be described as the government's willing mouthpiece: the visit of a government minister to some wretched village to harangue the peasants on the necessity of growing more food was the day's lead story, followed by a badly written account of the latest efforts by the authorities to stop cross-border cattle smuggling. Kabral watched me take it all in and then smiled: 'You believe what they told you?'

The pity of it was that the *Daily Graphic*, up until two years previously, was still considered the best paper in the country, although even then people were beginning to complain that its coverage of national affairs was insufficiently critical of the Rawlings regime. Their suspicions were confirmed when, in early 1986, an editorial appeared in support of a government order banning workers' leave allowances. The order was later rescinded after widespread industrial action and then it was discovered that the editorial had in fact been written by an official in the Castle Information Bureau, the government's main propaganda organ with an office in Osu Castle, the seat of government. It was headed, incongruously enough, by an Englishwoman married to a Ghanaian by the name of Valerie Sackey who was pointed out to me one day as she was being driven around central Accra in her official Land Rover. A subsequent meeting of the paper's staff passed a vote of no-confidence in the government-appointed editor. Predictably enough, the authorities resisted demands that he be removed. Such editors were perhaps better described as state-appointed bureaucrats whose task was not so much to report the news as to recycle bulletins handed down from the lofty heights of the Bureau, like so many civil servants faithfully carrying out government directives.

Government control of the media was especially evident in the work of the Ghana News Agency. If the size of a building alone is enough to change history, then the GNA would have been competing on equal terms with Reuters, TASS and Agence France-Presse, but an undertaking of this magnitude depended on more than just the outward symbols. Reporters must be able to report. As the Agency operated, all copy sent in from around the country had to be channelled through the office in Accra, where it was vetted before it was passed on to the local papers. Its head was a government appointee who knew what was and was not acceptable to their political masters.

The same treatment was given to reports from the outside agencies to which, in any case (and except for the American-owned Associated Press), only the Agency was permitted to subscribe. Some of the 'editing' was ludicrous and one wondered why they bothered. For example, any reference to supposedly fellow socialist countries like Zimbabwe and Ethiopia was always positive; the government of South Africa was always 'racist'. As regards the latter, the idea seemed to be that Ghanaian journalists might be in some doubt as to the evil nature of the regime and so must be alerted at every opportunity. The result was the inevitable debasement of language: when every reference to South Africa is prefixed by 'racist', then the word itself becomes meaningless.

The conclusion to be drawn from all this was that individual Ghanaians, but most especially the intellectuals, couldn't be trusted to interpret events in the 'correct' light, whether in their own country or abroad. This became sinister when you realised that the state had effectively determined that it alone had a monopoly on patriotism, and that anybody who challenged whatever interpretation it chose to give events was a traitor. Literally so, as I was to discover. And once this principle had been sufficiently established in the collective mind, the state then assumed the moral right—not to say moral duty—to incarcerate those who disagreed with it. The truth, of course, was quite the reverse. It was the imprisoned journalists who were the real patriots. One only had to listen to people like Kabral and Baako to see how much they loved their country, and how pained they were at what was happening to it. Unsurprisingly, domestic and foreign coverage in the Ghanaian media was not only outdated but appallingly inaccurate. During the week I spent there, I was reading about events which had occurred at least five days before and then at a double remove. As a result, nobody believed what they were told. Everywhere I went, and not only in Ghana but in Liberia, Sierra Leone and The Gambia, people tuned into the BBC and Voice of America to learn about the latest developments in their own country. So much for Nkrumah's vision: thirty years after decolonisation, Ghana continued to remain an outpost of empire, a dependent colony with only the appearance of independence.

Yet the curious thing about censorship in Ghana was that it didn't appear to be *for* any specific end. The authorities had a hazy notion of what they were *against*—American imperialism via Western multinationals—but it remained only at the level of rhetoric. This was especially ironic since the government had only recently invited the International Monetary Fund, that most capitalist of all institutions, to help solve the growing economic crisis: one needed a paper bag to carry the equivalent of £50, and this in a country which, at independence, was ahead of South Korea in terms of GDP. Indeed, at the time it had such a surplus of foreign exchange that it had even begun to build a nuclear reactor. It was as if the overthrow of Nkrumah by the military in 1966 left a vacuum in the intellectual life of the society that could only be filled by an increasing authoritarianism, which was itself a substitute for genuine thought, but which he had himself initiated by killing off democracy in his lust for power. But this wasn't the whole story, as I learnt when Kabral took me to see

Tommy Thompson, publisher of the *Free Press* until its voluntary closure. Twice imprisoned in 1985 without charge or trial, he was now tired.

'I've just turned sixty. I've got maybe twenty years, if I'm lucky. My wife has suffered enough, and my children need me more than ever.' He thought for a moment. 'Our journalists are partly to blame,' he continued. 'They aren't prepared to take risks. When I first started out, in the colonial days, we were ready to go to prison for what we believed in. That is what it means to be a journalist. The Nigerians understand this. They say what they feel, and they accept the consequences. Here we just have small boys who only want to make money and become known in society. They don't care about what is happening around them.'

In a way, it was unfair of Tommy Thompson to compare Ghana with Nigeria, countries so wide apart in terms of wealth, population and sheer energy as to constitute different worlds, then as now. But he was also right. Before leaving Lagos on another trip the following year, I had attended a symposium—sponsored, ironically enough, by the then military government—where Wọlé Ṣóyínká told the army in Africa to get out of politics and stay out. In his keynote address, he demanded that his fellow writers 'use their skill and exploit whatever strategies can be thought of for ending the uncertainty of social existence which is innate to the condition of the forcibly governed'; and added:

> A few months ago, I seized my opportunity to call for the abolition of the theocratic ideal in all forms of government... Today, I seize the occasion to invite the writers of this continent to join me in a complementary endeavour. The 'divine right of kings' which ended with the decapitation of crowned heads of Europe several centuries ago has—need I state the obvious?—been replaced by the 'divine right of the gun' on this continent. We must now invite all our dictatorships, under no matter what camouflage, and however comparatively civilianised

and domesticated they are—to set a definitive date within this century for the abandonment of this denigration of our popular will.[5]

Fighting words, to be sure; this and more was said in front of the country's second-in-command, Rear-Admiral Augustus Aikhomu, who sat on the podium looking increasingly alarmed. It may even have crossed his mind that such an unambiguous call to arms might be translated by the assembled delegates into immediate action, in which case his neck would certainly have been on the line; and there was no mistaking the look of relief that crossed his features when the critical moment passed.

Of course, as the country's only Nobel laureate Ṣóyínká was unassailable, a fact both he and Aikhomu were only too aware of. A less prominent person might have run into trouble although it is always foolish to underestimate any military government, especially in Nigeria, and this despite that regime's continual pronouncements regarding the necessity for a human rights policy, which may have been no more than a public relations exercise. There was still the suspicion, for instance, that it was this administration which assassinated Délé Gíwá, editor of the weekly *Newswatch* magazine, who was killed by a parcel bomb delivered to his home three days after he was visited by senior security officers. According to rumour (I say rumour: no one was ever held), Gíwá was told by one Gloria Okon, whom he had visited in London, that the wife of a certain person at the highest level was implicated in the escalating cocaine trade. He was working on the article at the time of his death, whereupon his lawyer, the late Chief Gani Fáwẹ̀hìnmi, was blocked at every turn in his attempt to uncover the truth and repeatedly detained on the flimsiest of excuses. On more than one occasion, he publicly expressed fears for his life.

Then there was the case of Patrick Wilmot, a West Indian lecturer who was kidnapped by the authorities on his way home one evening, driven overnight to Lagos airport and forcibly put on a flight to London. The authorities claimed that Wilmot, who had by then lived in Nigeria for over a decade and was married to a Nigerian, was a South African spy. In fact, he was a self-avowed Marxist—a dangerous admission in that climate, as another lecturer, the novelist Festus Iyayi, would subsequently discover—who had published a list of Nigerian companies, some of them headed by prominent government ministers, which were trading illegally with the apartheid state.

Yet, for all that, what was notable was the prominence Ṣóyínká's address received in the following day's newspapers. Even the government-owned *Daily Times*, hardly famous for its radical journalism, quoted from it extensively on its front page. More amusing still was to hear the staff at the National Theatre—the bartender and the waiter and the doorman—loudly discussing, with undisguised approval, the import of what Ṣóyínká had said. Such wide coverage of so damning a speech could never have occurred in Ghana, where, in 1989, Professor Adu Boahen, the historian, delivered a series of public lectures in Accra in which he castigated the Rawlings regime for subverting the society on the grounds that military rule *per se* was inimical to progress. Referring specifically to the culture of silence in which the independent press had been 'strangulated', he spoke of the resultant climate of fear that had been generated in the country: 'We are afraid of being detained, liquidated or dragged before the CVC [Citizens Vetting Committee] or the NIC [National Investigations Committee] or being subjected to all sorts of molestations.' He also called for more equity and justice, for the restoration of freedom of association and for the release of all political detainees. Although the distinguished professor was not invited for questioning or in any way physically harmed, the treatment his lectures received in the Ghanaian press contrasted with the Nigerian example. An 'editorial' in the *Daily Graphic*, for instance, claimed that he had 'at one time or another tried and failed in national politics' and that his lectures were 'full of mischief and provocation,' as though there were a logical and therefore damning connection between these two statements.[6]

The attempt to slur a person's character to undermine their argument can only ever be expressed in the crudest terms, but what always seems to escape those who try to do so is the all-too-obvious hysteria which only succeeds in defeating their purpose. One's instinctive reaction is always to disbelieve them, especially when they then proceed to engage in what amounts to a public vendetta: one week later, still apparently unable to leave the matter alone, the same paper carried a speech by a high-ranking military officer, General Quainoo, who repudiated the idea that the army was responsible for Ghana's present malaise and instead blamed those 'whose utterances and deeds showed that they are no patriots,' the implication obviously being that army generals were in the best position to decide who qualified as a patriot and who didn't. The general's speech was also carried in the *Ghanaian Times* over four consecutive days. Both reports, or editorials, or whatever they chose to call them, ended with what amounted to a death threat—or something that came suspiciously close to one: 'if those who engineer division and national disintegration, financiers behind the mercenary plots, and instigators of tribalism do not put an end to their nefarious and subversive activities, what will come next time will not be fire but an inferno, a conflagration.'[7]

Unfortunately for the general, all this was rather late in the day. The lectures created a sensation in Accra even though advertisements already paid for by the organisers failed to appear in any of the newspapers. On each of the three days of the lectures the spacious hall was packed to capacity. Those who couldn't get in gathered outside to listen on the PA system. And those who missed them altogether had no problem getting hold of the typescript, which ran to over seventy pages. It took me just twenty-four hours after arriving to locate a copy. Given all this, it was no mistake that Tommy Thompson looked back on the colonial period as a sort of Golden Age, or that one looks back on Nkrumah as the only Ghanaian leader with a vision. The nature of the colonial struggle, the dream of an independent Africa free from foreign domination, acted as a unifying force across the continent. It galvanised all sections of society and gave purpose to those actively engaged in ridding Africa of direct European rule with selected 'natives' given seats at the table but without a vote, much like the recent call for two African countries to be made permanent members of the UN Security Council but without veto powers. Every self-respecting journalist expected to go to prison for their beliefs and could count on the support of everybody but the foreign oppressor. But the struggle against colonialism was also reactionary in the strict sense: it was a reaction against somebody else's ideas of how the world worked, and it drew from the very tradition it fought against, from the ideas of Marx and Engels and Lenin imbibed in the very heart of Empire. It was from London, after all, that Nkrumah launched his campaign.

With independence achieved, the essential hollowness of the anti-colonial rhetoric resulted in an intellectual vacuum that could only be filled by naked power. When the armed forces struck in one country after another within the first decade, it wasn't the result of a specific programme but a failure of ideas. Authoritarian rule will only end in Africa when new ideas, African ideas, begin to determine the limits of power and the nature of political institutions. This is necessarily a long and painful process which we are only beginning to grapple with at a more serious level than hitherto, as I saw when I toured the region more than three decades later for this book.

*

But if the conditions for journalists in Ghana were bad, they were worse again in Liberia. The only country in the subregion that supposedly escaped the European 'scramble for Africa', it was settled by freed American slaves between 1820 and 1845 as a project of the American Colonisation Society, which believed—reasonably enough but wrongly, alas—that black people would face better chances for freedom and prosperity in the continent their forebears had been snatched from. Between 1822 and the outbreak of the American civil war in 1861, more than fifteen thousand freed and free-born African Americans, along with over three thousand Afro-Caribbeans, relocated to the 'Land of Freedom' and declared independence in 1847 (but which the US did not recognise until 1862).

During their long minority reign, which only ended with their overthrow in 1980, these so-called Americo-Liberians who 'retained preferences for Western style of dress, Southern plantation-style homes, American food, Protestantism, the English language, and monogamous kinship practices,'[8] allowed to be visited upon the natives—whom they termed 'aborigenes'—the plantation conditions they had left behind. In 1926, an American named Harvey Firestone Sr obtained—or 'wrested'—from the Liberian government a ninety-nine-year lease over one million acres, or roughly ten per cent of the country's arable land. This concession, which was secured in collusion with the US State Department, authorised the Ohio-based Firestone Tire & Rubber Company to cultivate millions of rubber trees, which made it both then and now the largest single natural rubber operation in the world. The project began with the forcible removal of indigenous communities and envisioned a workforce of 350,000, which was in effect the then total male indigenous population of working age. The company, for its part, trusted their 'brothers' in power to fill quotas that could never be met voluntarily, which they duly did by violently relocating thousands of workers, resulting in dozens of deaths. As early as 1928, a Harvard academic by the name of Raymond Leslie Buell concluded that the company was committing grave abuses given that the US State Department and Firestone had gained terms 'manifestly unfavourable' to the country. He further warned that 'conditions in Liberia' made forced labour 'almost inevitable' and argued that the impunity the company enjoyed surpassed even that of the colonial powers, which were at least 'responsible to European opinion' and therefore 'subject to some form of restraint'—which was as may be.[9]

Two years later, Marcus Garvey, the prominent Jamaican nationalist who was posthumously pardoned by the outgoing US president, Joe Biden, alerted the League of Nations—the precursor of the United Nations—that Firestone treated its Liberian labourers as 'virtual slaves'. In his opinion, this went against 'the best interests of Liberia, and the natives thereof, and the Negro race at large, for whom the Republic of Liberia was intended'. Together with the criticism from Buell, Firestone and the US State Department devised a 'pre-emptive strike', with US diplomats alleging that it was in fact the Liberian state which was practicing slavery. The League duly investigated and found the Americo-Liberian political elite guilty of forced labour and other practices akin to slavery, including coercing labourers to work on the plantation. The company itself was vindicated of any wrongdoing. Writing in 1933, W.E.B. Du Bois, the American scholar earlier alluded to, opined that Liberia was itself not 'faultless' given that 'her chief crime is to be black and poor in a rich, white world; and in precisely that portion of the world where colour is ruthlessly exploited as a foundation for American and European wealth.'[10] The country's punishment, he argued, was to suffer the company's depravations.

In 1980, the government of the increasingly minority Americo-Liberians—no more than five per cent of the population—was overthrown by Samuel Doe, a twenty-eight-year-old, semi-literate master-sergeant who caused thirteen of the deposed cabinet members to be executed on a public beach (and who was himself to suffer an even more gruesome and equally public fate less than a year after I left). From the start, he made his position on the press crystal clear, beginning with the *Daily Observer*, which quickly became the country's highest-selling newspaper when it was launched in early 1981. It was closed twice in its first year: for one month for publishing three letters on the government ban on student leaders, and then for two months for an article deploring the filthy state of the capital, Monrovia (itself named after the fifth US president, James Monroe). The paper was forcibly closed another three times over the next four years, culminating in a twenty-two-month ban in early 1985 when soldiers descended on the premises, ordered everybody out and padlocked the doors. This was in preparation for the forthcoming elections that were meant to transmute Doe from military dictator to civilian president at the behest of President Ronald Reagan, who had once welcomed his good friend 'Chairman Moe' to the White House, having earlier referred to 'those monkeys from those African countries... This bunch of people who don't even wear shoes yet, to be kicking the United States in the teeth,'[11] because the Tanzanian delegates had ululated on the UN floor in 1971 following the recognition of the People's Republic of China as the only legitimate representative of China. Their Nigerian counterparts—as with so many others, then as now—remained steadfast Obedient Boys of the Empire, being monkeys themselves.

The *Daily Observer* proprietors, meanwhile, were helpless to do anything following an earlier decree which made criticism of the government a criminal offence. One year later, Kenneth Best, the managing editor, decided to reopen on the grounds that the new, post-election constitution restored 'all the rights of the Liberian people, which may have been suspended during the years of military rule'. The following night, the offices were set ablaze and thousands of dollars' worth of equipment destroyed. It remained closed for more than a year until Doe, 'in the spirit of national unity and reconciliation,' lifted the ban in 1987.[12]

The experience of the *Daily Observer* was repeated with the other two independent papers: *Sun Times* and *Footprints Today*. The former was closed for two months, also in 1985, for hinting at possible government complicity in a banned opposition leader's motor accident. The offices of the latter were descended on by Doe's 'boys' brandishing steel chains and batons who warned the editor to 'stop publishing bad things about us'. The raid itself occurred only a matter of days before the paper's publisher, Momolu Sirleaf, and the sports editor, Klon Hinneh, were released from detention at the notorious Post Stockade, where they had been held incommunicado for two months. Both men had been detained for a month the previous year for publishing extracts from a confidential document about corruption in a government ministry, during which time they were flogged.

His treatment of the press aside, Doe was also reported to be mentally unstable even as he promoted himself to a five-star general. It didn't take long for rumours to abound of cannibalism inside the Executive Mansion, a practice which had featured in an article on a failed 1985 coup, 'How Quiwonkpa and Gbenyon died', that appeared in the (now defunct) *West Africa* magazine (23/30 December 1985):

> At the Barclay Training Ground, before hundreds of spectators, Quiwonkpa's body was chopped up into bits in a macabre cannibalistic ritual by some of Doe's soldiers who, astonishingly in these modern times, still believe that by eating bits of a great warrior's body, some of that greatness would come to them. The heart, of course, was the prize delicacy and it is traditionally shared on a hierarchical basis. The

blood-curdling dismemberment of Quiwonkpa was carried out in the open before hundreds of market women and shoppers who had trooped in from the Rally Time market to see if indeed Quiwonkpa had been killed. I personally saw two soldiers outside the Talk of the Town pub on Macdonald Street dangling what they said was Quiwonkpa's manhood. Other media colleagues reported seeing two fingers, presumably Quiwonkpa's, at Water Street, being dangled by jubilant soldiers who indicated they would devour their prize trophy at the end of the day.

Quiwonkpa, a Commanding General of the Armed Forces of Liberia, had come to prominence during the 1980 coup that brought Doe to power. He became part of Doe's Redemption Council, where he was promoted to Major-General but was purged in 1983 on suspicion of plotting a coup and forced into exile. He returned to the country in 1985 to overthrow Doe, counting on a popular uprising following the blatant election rigging that year 'marred by widespread intimidation of opposition parties and their candidates'. However, when it became clear that Doe was losing by a wide margin, he scrapped the legally prescribed Special Election Commission and appointed a fifty-member committee in its place composed almost exclusively of members of his severely minority Krahn ethnic group. The new committee 'recounted' the ballot papers in secret and came up with a more acceptable result. The following January, martial law gave way to a new constitution and Liberia was once more supposedly a democracy.

Charles Gbenyon, on the other hand, who was editor-in-chief of Liberian Television, had approached Doe for an interview at a public function a month after the aborted coup. On sighting him, the president screamed, 'Ain't you the one supporting Quiwonkpa? Take him away.' His security staff started beating him as he was ordered to strip to his underwear before he was handcuffed, thrown in the back of a jeep and driven to the

Executive Mansion in front of many eyewitnesses. A subsequent article, also in *West Africa*, described what happened:

> Gbenyon was ushered into Doe's first-floor office still only wearing his briefs. Never imagining that he had committed any offence...[he] innocently continued to protest that all he had done was in line with his professional responsibilities... When it appeared that the newsman was only grudgingly repentant for both the personal as well as the collective 'sin' of his 'Action Team' (of TV reporters) the Liberian leader told the guards to 'go fuck with him'.
>
> He was taken to the second floor and beaten unconscious. They later bayonetted him to death.

His corpse subsequently turned up on the beach, carefully arranged with his throat cut, head towards the sea and feet towards the mansion. In a subsequent briefing with members of the diplomatic corps at the Executive Mansion, Doe denied that there had been any secret executions but then blurted out 'except the journalist, Charles Gbenyon, who died right here' before realising his slip.

All of this fitted in with reports I read while preparing for my 1988 trip which portrayed a society held together by naked terror perpetrated on the citizens by a whole panoply of security agencies, including the 'elite' Israeli-trained Special Anti-Terrorist Unit. A particularly horrific case-study concerned the attack on the country's only university in 1984 when, in response to a peaceful demonstration, a detachment of two hundred soldiers killed 'an undetermined number' of students in an operation that lasted five days. The university was subsequently closed, and a number of lecturers fled overseas.

During my visit, I was fortunate to track down Rufus Darpoh (now late), whose newspaper, the *Sun Times*, had been closed yet again for allegedly publishing articles considered 'hostile' to the government, thereby 'creating tension and instability'. He was now working as editor at *The Herald*, a newly established paper sponsored by the Catholic Church; as Archbishop Michael K. Francis said to me when I paid him a courtesy visit: 'We must make the government understand that the respect for fundamental human rights is an absolute necessity in any civilised society.' The paper's headlines spoke for themselves: 'Suppression of Free Speech Fragments Society', 'Sycophancy in Liberian Media', 'Catholic Media Personnel Urged to be Assertive in Promoting Social Justice', were a few typical ones. Evidently, Doe preferred not to take on the Church, as the archbishop well knew, which was why the archbishop also declared 1989 the Year of Human Rights in Liberia, whether Doe would or not.

And yet—who could blame him?—Darpoh himself wasn't sure that he wanted the hassles any longer. He was weary of the sudden invitations to the Executive Mansion in the middle of the night:

> The last time I went, President Doe said: 'You journalists are careless with your lives.' How was I supposed to respond? He kept me there for three hours, during which time he told me that he himself was invincible; that even if somebody came into the room right then and opened fire with a machine gun he wouldn't be killed. He said that some people were trying to harm him with *juju* but they wouldn't succeed.[13]

Darpoh also confirmed that agents of state security were employed to report on the activities of journalists and even pointed one out in the restaurant where we were having lunch. I have to say he was a disappointing-looking spy who could more easily have passed for a harassed civil servant. He even pretended he hadn't seen us—I was the only white-looking person in the joint—until Darpoh called him over and introduced me as his friend from London who was writing a report on press freedom in the country. Well, I couldn't hide now!

Indeed, Darpoh was in the habit of constantly introducing me in this fashion. One day, he took me along to the Ministry of Information so that I could talk with some people at the Liberian News Agency. I spent half an hour listening to the familiar line concerning the absence of press freedom anywhere, 'including Britain and the United States', before I was rescued by Darpoh. On the way out, he asked me if I was interested in meeting Emmanuel Bowier, the minister himself. This was more than I could have hoped for but in Darpoh's company no appointment was necessary. We walked straight past the waiting supplicants and into the minister's office, who was understandably flustered by our unexpected intrusion.

'In my student days, I used to be radical, you know, but with my new responsibilities...' he blurted out as he swept his hand over the files piled high on his desk. He was a young man, not yet forty, as were all the ministers in Doe's cabinet, and I liked him for his uneasiness. I was eventually to meet other ministers, for instance the minister for planning and economic affairs, Dr Elijah Taylor, who was desperate that I admire the new compact disc player (yes, that long ago!) which he had bought for his new Mercedes Benz.

'Of course,' I said, 'you now have a new set of responsibilities,' and added: 'I must tell you that Rufus is the doyen of Liberian journalists. To us in London, he *is* Liberian journalism.'

The minister laughed. 'Yes, yes, I know,' he said, then glanced at his watch and started gathering files. 'But I have to go, the president is expecting me, and I am already late.'

I was tempted to ask him about this business of government agents spying on the media, but afterwards I spoke with another, younger journalist who repeated Darpoh's charge. This journalist, who had been detained at least once in the past, and who had agreed to speak with me on condition of anonymity, was so wary of associating with a foreigner that he lowered his voice throughout our interview and kept glancing over his shoulder. I didn't think that his fear was exaggerated or that he was indulging in histrionics. He went further. He said that since his imprisonment at Post Stockade, his telephone was tapped, and he was sometimes followed for days at a time as he went about his work.

Hysteria came naturally to the visitor to Liberia in those days. People spoke incessantly of hearing screams emanating from the Executive Mansion in the dead of night. It wasn't shameful to fear for one's life in an environment which hadn't changed since Graham Greene's *Journey Without Maps* half-a-century earlier:

> 'But no,' Mr Nelson said, turning his yellow, malicious eyes over the pointed leaking huts, 'we don't like Faulkner.' After a while, he found enough vitality to explain. 'You see, he has an idea.'
> 'What idea?' I said.
> 'Nobody knows,' Mr Nelson said, 'but we don't like it.'

What I didn't know at the time was that the country was about to descend into a twelve-year civil war. Indeed, the forces under Charles Taylor, the soon-to-be-notorious warlord and himself an Americo-Liberian who had served in Doe's first cabinet before they fell out, were just then amassing on the eastern border with Côte d'Ivoire. They would invade just one month after I left for Sierra Leone on the western border, and which was itself to be consumed in its own, parallel civil war just one year after Liberia's as a direct consequence of it.

Following in the footsteps of Ghana under Nkrumah, Sierra Leone officially became a one-party state in 1978 when Dr Siaka Stevens secured more than the two-thirds majority in the House of Representatives to rewrite the constitution. Already in power ten years by then, he eventually retired in 1985 and anointed Major-General Joseph Saidu Momoh his successor as reward for his unflinching loyalty, having quashed at least one attempted military coup against him. Momoh was equally well regarded in his chosen profession—he was best overseas cadet at the Mons Officer Cadet School in Aldershot, England—but was politically naive. He had also inherited an economic mess—hence Stevens's resignation—although Sierra Leone was hardly alone in this.

The country's problem is the wider one which plagues a continent that has thirty per cent of the world's mineral resources (including forty per cent of the gold and up to ninety per cent of chromium and platinum) and pays the price accordingly.[14]

Regarding contemporary Sierra Leone, its exceptionally high-quality diamonds were first discovered by the British colonial government in the 1930s. Exclusive mining rights were granted to the South African De Beers Diamond Consortium and the profits shared between British and European shareholders, with the locals only benefitting from regular (if badly paid) employment and the infrastructure necessary to transport the produce to the coast. However, because the diamonds were commonly dispersed close to the surface or riverbeds and could be mined by anyone with a shovel and a sieve, it didn't take long for an illegal trade to flourish, with a strong pipeline established between Sierra Leone and Liberia largely dominated by Lebanese traders. This decline continued under Siaka Stevens, who encouraged illicit mining during his tenure which he weaponised to 'settle' (Nigerian parlance) those he depended upon to remain in power. He also nationalised the diamond mines, including those run by De Beers. They were quickly replaced by an influx of Israeli investors with ties to Antwerp, the centre of the global diamond market, but the lack of proper standards—specifically, that the country of origin was the one it was held to have been exported from—meant they could smuggle diamonds into Liberia before selling them on to European buyers, thereby foregoing any duties in the originating country.

In Sierra Leone, meanwhile, the same diamonds were to become the centre of a civil war that was to erupt one year after the one in the same Liberia that was the conduit for those diamonds, and this despite the assurances of the warlord, Foday Sankoh, with a 'vision' for the 'people' who remained in dire poverty because of those very diamonds. But all that was to come. At the time of my first visit, Freetown itself, with just over half-a-million people, had a population less than half that of Monrovia although the country itself had twice as many people as its neighbour. Unlike Liberia, there were no daily newspapers; of the sixteen weeklies or fortnightlies, all but two of them were small-scale independent publications owned and edited by the proprietors themselves. The market they operated in was restricted by the thirty per cent literacy rate (about the same as Liberia), a melancholy fact for a country whose capital was once known as 'the Athens of West Africa', hosting as it did Fourah Bay College. Originally founded in 1827 as an Anglican missionary school by the Church Missionary Society, it was affiliated with Durham University from 1876 until 1967 and was for many decades the only institute of higher learning in the whole of British-ruled West Africa: Nigeria's University College of Ibadan (now University of Ibadan), and Ghana's University College of the Gold Coast (now University of Ghana), were only founded in 1948.

On that my first visit, I stayed with the pipe-smoking poet and novelist Syl Cheney-Coker. He had only recently returned home with his Filipina wife and their ten-year-old daughter after a teaching stint in a Nigerian university in the days when that country's naira still garnered some respect, and with which he was able to build a modest bungalow overlooking a river on the outskirts of Freetown, from the veranda of which we sipped beers in the fading light as we watched the fishermen row by in their wooden canoes. He was then publishing one of the best newspapers, *The Vanguard*, a fortnightly. If I say that it was a labour of love, I mean that he lost on each issue. It took three days to produce a mere two thousand copies, the maximum he could manage, even though he could easily have sold three or four times that number. Every stage of production was a headache. The paper on which it was printed was begged from a friend in the French embassy; the plates were set in the government printing department through the good offices of an old classmate; the printing itself was done as a favour by an acquaintance who could earn twice as much by sticking to more commercial jobs: invitation cards for the Indian Association, wedding invitations for the Lebanese community, calling cards for budding business people. This was to say nothing of the constant power failures which, for one frustrating afternoon, stopped the presses rolling for three hours. By the end of it, as we scrutinised the finished product, I hope that I managed to communicate my admiration for his guts and determination. He said: 'At some future date, when things finally get impossible and I'm forced to fold, I want it to be said that at least one person tried to produce a worthwhile newspaper.' That was to happen soon enough when he and his family were forced to flee the country as the civil war closed in on Freetown and destroyed his bungalow. He eventually ended up in the US, where he currently lives; in the meantime, he wasn't going to give up without a fight. In his regular column, 'Editor's notebook', he had written:

> Many years ago, I gave up on this country. I turned my back on its needless trivialities that were becoming fashionable among the generation now in power. Without realizing it we had preceded by a few years the age of the Yuppies. We measured everything by the primacy of wealth, business connections and positions. Ideas went out of the window like discarded baggage. We were in a hurry to join the age of moral bankruptcy.

But at least he managed to evade the wrath of Momoh, for whom 'the journalist's pen is as lethal as the rifle in the hand of a military marksman,' but which, he hastened to add, didn't mean that they 'should not criticise,' provided only that 'the criticism is objective'. Paul Kamara, editor of *For Di People*, unfortunately fell short of that ideal. First detained under Dr Stevens for several weeks for publishing a letter about the alleged sale of a super-carat diamond by a government official, he was arrested twice under Momoh, the first for an article critical of the strong-arm tactics of the military police, the second the year before I visited for an article accusing a well-known Lebanese family of short-changing the government on contracts it hadn't properly fulfilled. It seems it had purchased second-hand power generators unsuitable for the tropics which were forever breaking down and plunging the country into darkness (at least in those areas they purported to serve) and then failed to provide twenty-two tractors for the 'green revolution' that was supposed to transform the country's agriculture.

A few days after this was published, a bailiff called at Kamara's house and told him that a friend of his from the Criminal Investigations Department was parked nearby and wanted a word. As soon as he stepped outside, the bailiff waved a piece of paper he claimed was a warrant for his arrest. This later proved to be a forgery, but he was bundled into the car before he could examine it and driven to the by-now familiar Pademba Road Prison. He was left in a cell for four days before he was brought before a magistrate on a charge of criminal libel. Bail was set at an impossible half-a-million leones, but he was freed the following day when an anonymous benefactor put up the money. Kamara's lawyer then brought a counteraction against the Lebanese family, but the magistrate said that she had received instructions from the director of public prosecutions that the family shouldn't be prosecuted. Meanwhile, Kamara was having trouble finding a printer for the entire period the case dragged. In the end, he was forced to settle out of court by agreeing to print an apology. But all this paled into insignificance when the civil war just breaking out in Liberia spilled over into Sierra Leone, with possibly even more devastating consequences.

4

THE STOLEN PEOPLE

Freetown was first settled in 1787 by 400 former slaves freed during the American Revolutionary War. Evacuated first to London, they were sent on from there under the auspices of the Committee for the Relief of the Black Poor, an organisation set up by Granville Sharp, the British abolitionist. Of these, all but about sixty-four died from disease and clashes with the indigenes who resented their presence. From 1808 to 1874, the city served as the capital of British West Africa as well as the base for the Royal Navy's West Africa Squadron charged with enforcing the ban on the slave trade. Altogether, the squadron seized about 1,600 slaving ships, freeing about 150,000 people as proof of the civilising mission of a benign British Empire upon which the sun never set but not before compensating the 47,000 slave-owning individuals and families to the tune of £20 million (£16.5 billion today, representing forty per cent of the Treasury's tax receipts at the time) for the loss of their 'property'. The property, in turn, not only got nothing but were made to work as 'apprentices'—for free—for another four years. The reparations, which was what it amounted to in light of the current agitation for the descendants of the slaves to be similarly compensated, was only paid off in 2015, courtesy of the British taxpayers who were themselves enslaved in the interests of the landowning aristocracy which persists till today. The family of David Cameron, the former Conservative prime minister, was among the recipients of the largesse, as was that of William Gladstone, his Liberal predecessor, whose father, Sir John Gladstone, 1st Baronet, received the largest payout (over £10 million at today's rates) for the loss of 2,508 slaves across nine plantations. Also included were the families of George Orwell and Graham Greene, although I'm sure they would both have been mortified if they had known during their lifetimes.

But it is in The Gambia that the slave trade's impact on the geography of a country is most keenly felt. The smallest on the African mainland—its widest part is just thirty miles—its total area is slightly bigger than Jamaica, or twice that of Delaware in the United States. It is also unusual in being surrounded on three sides by another country—Senegal—although it has its own coastline with the Atlantic Ocean. It was from here that an estimated three million slaves—about five thousand a year—were transported from an island about four hours by boat off the coast of Banjul, the current capital. First 'discovered' by the Portuguese in 1456, it was initially known as Andrew Island but then renamed James Island (after King James II of England) following its capture by the English in 1661.

In 2011, it was renamed Kunta Kinteh Island following a request from New York artist Chaz Guest to Gambian President Yahya Jammeh to give it a Gambian name, after the character in Alex Haley's bestselling book, *Roots: The Saga of an American Family*, a semi-fictionalised account of his own family history. The island, now listed as a UN World Heritage Site, could hold up to six hundred captives at any one time but has suffered heavy erosion over the centuries and is currently one-sixth of its original size. It contains several of the British administrative structures, including a single cell for the more 'troublesome' captives, along with a small jetty. There are also a few forlorn-looking baobab trees, a unique species that can tolerate many environments but perhaps the island was too humid. It was only when I turned east into the dry, dusty Sahelian countries on the edge of the Sahara—Mali, Burkina Faso, Niger—that these long-lived giants of many parts revealed themselves in all their splendour, of which more anon.

According to Haley's novel, Kunta Kinte lived a carefree life in the village of Jufureh by the River Gambia. Sometimes there was not enough food to eat because his parents were subsistence farmers in a harsh climate. As time passed, he began to hear about the toubob, the white-skinned slavers with their 'wet chicken smells' who burned down villages, killed those deemed unfit and carted away the rest to the island to await transportation. As it happens, Kunta's father, Omoro, once accompanied his two brothers 'to see what the toubob were doing, to see what might be done'. They trekked for three days, 'keeping carefully concealed in the bush, until they find what they are looking for,' to wit:

> ...stolen people chained inside long, heavily guarded bamboo pens along the shore of the river. When small canoes brought important-acting toubob from the big canoes, the stolen people were dragged outside their pens onto the sand.
> 'Their heads had been shaved, and they had been greased until they shined all over. First they were made to squat and jump up and down,' said Omoro. 'And then when the toubob had seen enough of that, they ordered the stolen people's mouths forced open for their teeth and their throats to be looked at.'
> Swiftly, Omoro's finger touched Kunta's crotch, and as Kunta jumped, Omoro said, 'Then the men's private foto was pulled and looked at. Even the women's private parts were inspected.' And the

> toubob finally made the people squat again and stuck burning hot irons against their backs and shoulders. Then, screaming and struggling, the people were shipped towards the water, where small canoes waited to take them out to the big canoes.
>
> 'My brothers and I watched many fall onto their bellies, clawing and eating the sand, as if to get one last hold and bite of their own home,' said Omoro. 'But they were dragged and beaten on.' Even in the small canoes out in the water, he told Kunta and Lamin, some kept fighting against the whips and the clubs until they jumped into the water among terrible long fish with grey backs and white bellies and curved mouths full of thrashing teeth that reddened the water with their blood.'
>
> Kunta and Lamin had huddled closer to each other, each gripping the other's hands. 'It's better that you know these things than that your mother and I kill the white cock one day for you.'[1]

He relates all this to Kunta and his younger brother as a warning against being taken unawares, especially since their own people, 'slatee traitors', work for the toubob but that, unfortunately, 'there is no way to recognize them' for who they are.

And where were they taken to? 'The elders say to Jong Sang Doo,' said Omoro, 'a land where slaves are sold to huge cannibals called toubabo koomi, who eat us. No man knows any more about it.' This apparently contrasted with the more benign version of indigenous slavery:

> Omoro said that people became slaves in different ways. Some were born of slave mothers—and he named a few of those who lived in Juffure whom Kunta knew well. Some of them were the parents of some of his own kafo mates. Others, said Omoro, had once faced starvation during their home villages' hungry season, and they had come to Juffure and begged to become the slaves of someone who agreed to feed and provide for them. Still others—and he named some of Juffure's older people—had once been enemies and been captured

as prisoners. 'They became slaves, being not brave enough to die rather than be taken,' said Omoro.

All had '[t]heir rights guaranteed by the laws of our forefathers', including 'food, clothing, a farm plot to work on half shares, and also a wife or husband,' and could eventually buy their freedom. Indeed, it was only those 'who permit themselves to be...despised,' who could be done with what their masters will, excepting 'convicted murderers, thieves, or other criminals,' who 'were the only slaves whom a master could beat or otherwise punish, as he felt they deserved.' But the idea, common enough, that one type of slavery is better than another would seem to be a contradiction in terms—a slave is a slave is a slave—but is continuously touted in West Africa generally as proof of the white man's especial depravity, based as it is on the concept of 'race' that is really the legend of colour that we still find difficult to overcome but which we shall, Lord, we surely shall; as James Baldwin put it: 'the value placed on the colour of the skin is always and everywhere and forever a delusion.'

But let us not get too abstract. If you want to know how indigenous slaves were treated in those days, look at how 'houseboys' and 'house girls' are treated in Nigeria in these days:

> In 2020, State Criminal Investigation and Intelligence Department operatives arrested Franc Ifedili and Ifunnanya Ifedili after the police received a petition from the human rights organization, Paths of Peace Initiatives, about the inhumane treatment suffered by the victim. The organization charges that the couple were 'in the habit of bringing minors from villages to act as house boys and girls, subjecting them to all sorts of child abuse including corporal punishments and others.' In reference to Nmesso, a 9-year-old whom they brought to live and work as a house girl, it became evident that 'she was subjected to all sorts of inhuman maltreatment including daily flogging (by horsewhip).' When Nmesso fled, the Ifedilis brought another minor, Chidera, a

9-year-old boy whom they have subjected to flogging and other similar treatment suffered by Nmesso. As recent[ly] as June 2020, the Lagos State Police continued to investigate the couple for allegedly abusing Chidera. Stories such as this have prompted celebrities and others to publicly admonish those who employ child domestic servants.[2]

Stories like this are repeated ad nauseam, and not only in Nigeria but among wealthy Nigerians abroad (and indeed, the subregion generally). One such case in 2024 involved a young woman called Rose who was taken to London on the promise that she would continue with her education, instead of which she was made to work twelve hours a day, six days a week in the restaurant the couple ran; on the seventh day she did all the house chores. 'That's when it dawned on me, oh, these people actually bring me here to work for them as a slave.' She said the couple constantly shouted at her, calling her 'stupid' and 'useless'. Once, the wife slapped her for a perceived act of disobedience: 'My life was hell.' Worse was to come when the wife travelled, leaving her at the mercy of the husband. 'The man abused me in so many ways. Sexually, emotionally, physically. He raped me countless times because I can't talk to anybody.'[3]

Rape, of course, is a corollary of slavery. In *Roots*, Kunta witnessed a young woman being kidnapped. She later returned and gave birth to a mulatto child before Kunta was himself ambushed along with others and taken to the island where they were stripped naked, examined in every orifice, chained and burned with hot irons before they were placed in the brig of a ship. After the nightmarish, five-thousand-mile journey across the Atlantic, he and those others who survived the middle passage landed in Annapolis, Maryland, where he was purchased by one John Waller at an auction and given the name Toby. Kunta, who was headstrong, attempted to run away four separate times; on the last occasion, part of his right foot was amputated to ensure that he didn't try again. By and by, he became a gardener and then his master's buggy driver. Following the American Revolution, he married a woman named Bell, Waller's cook, with whom he had a daughter, Kizzy. She had a relatively happy childhood until she forged a travelling pass for her intended, a field hand who was caught and confessed, whereupon she was sold away from her family at the age of sixteen to Tom Lea, a farmer and chicken fighter, who raped her. She gave birth to George, who turned out to be a philanderer known for his expensive tastes and love of alcohol. George married Matilda, who gave him six sons and two daughters, including Tom, who became a blacksmith and married Irene, a woman originally owned by the Holt family. After Tom Lea lost all his money, most of the family were sold off to the Murrays in North Carolina but, following the civil war and now ostensibly free, they moved to Tennessee, which was looking for new settlers and where they eventually prospered. Tom's daughter, Cynthia, married Will Palmer, a successful lumber businessman; their daughter, Bertha, was the first person in the family to go to college, where she met Simon Haley and gave birth to Alex, the author of the book we are reading.

As Haley later explained, 'every lineage statement within *Roots* is from either my African or American families' carefully preserved oral history, much of which I have been able conventionally to corroborate with documents'; and he added, 'Those documents, along with the myriad textural details of what were contemporary indigenous lifestyles, cultural history, and such that give *Roots* flesh have come from years of intensive research in fifty-odd libraries, archives, and other repositories on three continents.' For instance, in the US census for Alamance County in North Carolina, he found evidence of Tom Murray, the blacksmith. He also attempted to locate the likeliest origin of the African words passed down by Kunta Kinte, notably kora, a stringed instrument in the Mandinka language, and bolongo, river. Haley then travelled to The Gambia, where he learnt about griots, the oral historians trained from childhood to memorise the history of a particular village; a good one can speak for three days without repeating themselves. He asked to hear the history of the Kinte clan and was taken to a griot named Kebba Kanji Fofana. It seems that the clan had originated in Old Mali and moved to Mauritania before settling in The Gambia. Kunta, the eldest of four sons, went in search of wood one day and was never seen again. Haley then went to the UK where, in Lloyd's of London, he discovered that a slave ship by the name of *Lord Ligonier* had sailed from The Gambia on 5 July 1767 bound for Annapolis, where it cleared customs on 29 September 1767; the slaves were advertised for auction in the *Maryland Gazette* on 1 October 1767. Finally, he examined the deed books of Spotsylvania County after September 1767 and located one dated 5 September 1768 transferring 240 acres and a slave named Toby from John and Ann Waller to William Waller.

The book itself was a great success; it sold over fifteen million hardback copies within seven months and won a Pulitzer Prize. '*Roots* meant so much to so many people. I mean you have to understand that in a lot of households, a copy of the book was placed right next to the Bible on family coffee tables. I can vouch for this because that's what it was like when I was growing up,' according to the academic Kellie Carter Jackson, who edited a book of essays, *Reconsidering Roots*, on the fortieth anniversary of its publication. She was exercised by the fact that the tepid prose of the most popular book by an African American writer was spurned by intellectuals, who considered Haley 'lowbrow' because he 'wrote for *Playboy*' and was 'always looking for ways to make money'. That is to say, he was a professional writer and not a tenured professor, much like James Baldwin, for instance, who also wrote for *Playboy*, as did Margaret Atwood, Gabriel García Márquez, Ursula Le Guin, Vladimir Nabokov,

Joyce Carol Oates... (Spoiler alert: the magazine pays top-notch, and writers, like everyone else, also need to eat.) And then it transpired that the professors were right, at least in part: he had indeed plagiarised large parts of Harold Courlander's 1967 novel, *The African*, and settled the case out of court for $650,000 (over $3 million today). It also happened at the time that 'academics all across the country were just starting to get their own Africana studies programs off the ground, and this plagiarism scandal delivered a blow to their legitimacy'.[4]

Further doubts were raised about the factual evidence Haley claimed to rely on. In a *Sunday Times* article, 'Tangled Roots', Mark Ottaway challenged the book's account of Kunta Kinte himself. The problem was that the only confirmation of Haley's family history came from a griot who was not considered genuine by his own community, and who kept changing key details with each retelling. Moreover, a historian of the slave trade, Donald R. Wright, claimed that griots in The Gambia could not provide detailed information on people living before the mid-nineteenth century, and the only reason that everyone heard about Kunta Kinte in the first place was because Haley himself kept repeating the story on his visits to 'black West Africa' (in Haley's own phrasing, as if there were a 'white West Africa') so that his version had at last been assimilated into the oral tradition; that, indeed, Haley had created a case of 'circular reporting' in which his story was simply repeated back to him.

There were other anomalies, beginning with the date showing that the Waller family already owned the slave Toby five years before his ship supposedly landed at Annapolis. Dr Waller didn't have a cook named Bell or his own plantation because he was disabled and lived with his brother, John. Toby seems to have died eight years before his daughter Kizzy was supposedly born. 'Missy' Anne could not have been Kizzy's childhood playmate as Ann Murray was a grown, married woman and there was no record of a Kizzy being owned by any of the Waller family. And so on. Haley himself conceded that his African research may have misled him, which was why he had initially thought of calling it a 'historical novel', but does any of it really matter? According to Professor Henry Louis Gates Jr, Haley's close friend: 'Most of us feel it's highly unlikely that Alex found the village whence his ancestors sprang. *Roots* is a work of the imagination rather than strict historical scholarship. It was an important event because it captured everyone's imagination.'[5] Indeed, one might argue that interrogating the historicity of the narrative deflects from the obscenity of the institution that was Haley's target: truth of mood, not fact, although one might legitimately take issue with the abundance of women's breasts in the first part of the equally popular televised series set in Africa (not Haley's fault), as indeed they also featured in Werner Herzog's *Cobra Verde*, the film of Bruce Chatwin's *The Viceroy of Ouidah* earlier alluded to.

The abundance of female flesh might have been excusable in the case of Chatwin's novel, given the mythology surrounding the so-called Amazons in the then Kingdom of Dahomey (modern-day Benin). The only all-female army in modern history, they were so named by the European slave traders who saw them as the warriors of Greek mythology. Indeed, their emergence as a 3,000-strong legion in the seventeenth century was the direct result of the dearth of male recruits following the incessant wars between Dahomey and the Oyo Empire in what became neighbouring Nigeria for male slaves to sell to these same Europeans. Their bravery was reflected in Marvel's blockbuster film *Black Panther*, and as the fictional Dora Milaje, the elite women warriors who protected the king of Wakanda. They were also reputed to have fought bare-chested although there is no evidence of this. Indeed, a photograph from the 1890s shows them fully covered up, with at least one account testifying that they 'wore brown blouses and brown-and-blue knee-length shorts'. And according to the 'academic renegade' Pamela Toler, author of *Women Warriors: An Unexpected History*:

> By the 1800s, contemporary accounts of them is that their uniforms were so similar to their male counterparts, people fighting against them don't realise they're women until they're up close in hand-to-hand combat. They most likely wore long shorts, a tunic, and a cap, not the sexualized almost bathing suits you'd see in modern-day depictions of female warriors.[6]

The point, in any case, is that no popular movies show a similar abundance of white breasts for reasons we needn't overlabour, although—figuratively speaking—any number can now be seen on the beaches of Banjul, as I observed during my first visit to the country.

5

THE ARMY THAT TRUMPETS THE DEMOCRATIC CALL

At the time of my first visit, The Gambia had been ruled since independence in 1965 by Alhaji Sir Dawda Jawara and differed from the other Anglophone countries in still being a functioning multiparty democracy, although Jammeh himself survived an attempted coup in 1981 which was put down by troops from Senegal (he wouldn't survive a second one twelve years later). The country's stability at the time was reflected not only in the fact that Banjul was chosen to host the 1989 Organisation of African Unity's African Commission on Human and Peoples' Rights, but that the problems of the independent press were largely the result of the twenty per cent literacy rate in a population of just over half-a-million (now standing at 2.7 million). One editor I spoke with complained that those with money didn't understand the economics of newspaper publishing and therefore didn't invest in the press, but the real problem was that they might have understood it only too well: 500 copies of a weekly, fortnightly or monthly—there was no daily, significantly enough—was simply not a viable business proposition. According to Momodou Faal, editor of *The Toiler*, a fourteen-page monthly, printing paper alone for 600 copies accounted for a third of his costs. Given that he also employed four staff, it was difficult to see how the paper managed to break even; and although he assured me that 'the organ of The Gambian Workers' Confederation had no political associations of any kind,' it was equally difficult to believe that it didn't receive subventions. Such was the case with *Foroyaa* (Freedom), for instance, one of whose editors confirmed that it had been set up three years earlier as the mouthpiece of the opposition People's Democratic Organisation for Independence and Socialism.

This is not to suggest that that there is anything particularly sinister in a paper's politics, or that the integrity of such a paper is in doubt merely because of that, but that an independent paper, properly defined, operates outside any such considerations. According to this definition, there were only two papers in The Gambia at the time which qualified as such: *The Nation*, a fortnightly edited by William Dixon-Colley; and *The Torch*, a weekly edited by Sanna Manneh. The former—'We try to be radical and pin down government on its policies,' he told me—worked within such tight margins that the seven sheets of each issue were first typed onto stencil and then laboriously stapled together by the editor himself. The latter had ceased publication the previous year following a libel action brought against the editor which bankrupted him.

The article in question openly accused four government ministers of corruption and recommended that they be sacked. Three of them promptly took the matter to court (the fourth wisely declined) and Manneh was charged with libel against each of the plaintiffs. *Foroyaa*, which printed special supplements throughout the five-month trial giving verbatim reports of the court proceedings, called it 'a landmark in Gambian political, legal and press history'. Manneh was eventually acquitted on two counts and cautioned and discharged on the third but was sceptical of ever publishing again when I met up with him. Be that as it may, the trial demonstrated that the government was prepared to allow the law to take its course, and this despite Manneh's initial difficulty in securing the services of a barrister and his apprehension that he would receive a fair trial. There was no reason to disagree with the summary of a journalist who declared himself satisfied that 'the trial reinforced the confidence of Gambians in their judicial system,' a view which was echoed in an editorial in *The Toiler*: 'It is indeed an historic case which in a way was testing the independence, fairness and astuteness of our judiciary in a tricameral system of political democracy... [It] not only acts to safeguard the human rights of citizens...but it also avoids corruption.'

And yet a cautious note was struck in an article in *The Nation* reporting Manneh's acquittal: 'News is spreading fast that certain groups, including civil servants, plan to send thugs against the editor of *The Torch* and other journalists.' In the event, nothing happened but Manneh insisted to me that he had been 'continually harassed' by men he didn't know. He was reluctant to say too much, and he didn't specify how they had harassed him, but he did say that his flat was broken into on more than one occasion and that papers had been removed. Even as we spoke, he indicated two young men on a bench at the bus stop across the road. He said that they had been following him about ever since the case had started. They turned away when I looked over at them, but missed the next two buses and were still there when we left.

With only one exception, of which more later, all evidence of direct government interference in the media was based on rumour, suspicion or simple deduction. In his 'As I See It' column, Dixon-Colley questioned the impartiality of Radio Gambia in covering certain issues, specifically its failure to report the libel case against *The Torch*: 'It is ridiculous that while the local press and the international news media have carried it, Radio Gambia chose not to mention it. Coincidentally, the Radio went off air the very day the judgment was delivered.' It also alleged that the order came directly from said minister. I later spoke to some staff at the station, but they denied that this was so. Dixon-Colley himself told me that during the case he had problems getting his paper printed. The head of the government printing press, the only printing press in the country, told him that the minister had forbidden him from printing the mastheads of the independent papers. Dixon-Colley demanded to see his written instructions, as provided for in law, but he claimed he had not been given any. When questioned, the minister denied that he had given any such instructions. However, as Dixon-Colley pointed out, the printer, who went ahead and printed anyway, had no motive for lying.

If either of the allegations against the minister was true, then he had been guilty of abuse of power. Neither constituted evidence of official complicity to silence the media, and Dixon-Colley was not alone in wondering whether the president himself was always aware of his minister's possible transgressions. Nonetheless, at the beginning of the trial the president had agreed that the charges were indeed serious and that, if true, those concerned 'will face the music', and his subsequent prevarications in a BBC interview disappointed many when he muttered something about waiting for the appeal to run its course given that 'we are talking about the reputation of individual ministers...that is extremely important'. Then again, two-and-a-half decades in power had perhaps blunted his judgment. No single individual should remain at the helm for so long, however 'democratically' elected, but then his was small beer compared with, say, the ninety-two-year-old Paul Biya of Cameroon, in power since 1975 and still there at the time of writing (although there are rumours that he may in fact be dead, given that he doesn't even live in the country, which he only visits at five-year intervals to cast his vote in an election he invariably wins). Mo Ibrahim, the Sudanese-British businessman and philanthropist, put it well in 2018 in the context of the then ninety-four-year-old Robert Mugabe of Zimbabwe seeking re-election after thirty-three years in power:

> We see people in wheelchairs unable to raise hands, standing for elections. This is a joke. Yes, you are right to laugh because the whole world is laughing at us... Obama, who happens to be half African anyway, became president when he was forty-six, forty-seven years old... If Obama was in Kenya, what would he be doing now? He would be driving a bus maybe... Why these big countries...entrust their economies, their nuclear weapons, all resources to people who are in their forties, and we only pick up people at ninety years old to lead us? To lead us where? To the grave?[1]

In 2007, Ibrahim set up a foundation to reward former heads of state for excellence in leadership up to three years after leaving office. Nelson Mandela was the obvious first choice but, unsurprisingly, it was only awarded five more times over the next seventeen years and, even then, raised eyebrows in at least one case.

Unfortunately, the end of Jawara in 1994 was also the end of democracy as The Gambia succumbed to the regional imperative in the person of the twenty-nine-year-old Lt. Yahya Jammeh, head of the Armed Forces Provisional Ruling Council. He was to sit tight for the next twenty-two years, first as a military dictator and then as a civilian president following elections in 2001. During his time in power, he declared The Gambia to be an Islamic state—about ninety-five per cent of the population is Muslim, which is why the abundance of female breasts in the *Roots* film is so unlikely—and withdrew from the Commonwealth. He did this on the grounds that the country 'will never be a member of any neo-colonial institution and will never be a party to any institution that represents an extension of colonialism,' which was true enough of the organisation but then he might have just been playing to the gallery. He finally relinquished power following his loss in the 2016 election (but only after an ECOWAS force was sent to help him on his way) and was succeeded by Adama Barrow of the main opposition United Democratic Party. The new president quickly rejoined the Commonwealth and un-Islamised the country, as it were.

In all of this, what hadn't changed between my first visit and this, my latest one, was the over one hundred thousand, mostly middle-aged and elderly Brits out for sun and sex—with women leading the way. On that my first visit, it was difficult to ignore the desperate young men clustered around the then five upmarket hotels with their private beachfronts—they have greatly multiplied since—waiting to be identified by their benefactors before they were admitted as the others looked on with envy. There is nothing hidden about the trade, which can be viewed on any number of YouTube posts, for instance 'The British Grannies on Gambian Men: Granbia'. There is fifty-year-old P, for instance, who visits three or four times a year for both the gorgeous tropical weather and 'a different man every night' should she so desire. She eventually meets the one of her dreams and gets married, following in the footsteps of her friend, fifty-eight-year-old Michelle, who had married her forty-six-year-old paramour two years previously who himself claimed to have single-handedly built their €80,000 Italian-style villa from the proceeds of his work as a plumber in the president's office.

More honest is thirty-two-year-old Alka, whose sixty-eight-year-old love of his life—'I want her to die in my arms'—sent him €60,000 for their own love nest on top of the €300 monthly stipend (nice work if you can get it) to help feed his seven juniors, along with his eighty-seven-year-old mother who knows nothing of her son's intended. As the fifty-seven-year-old Jackie remarks, the young men 'class it as a job. They are good at talking.' Indeed, Alka claimed he had been at it for fifteen years before his big break. Patience was all, he said, as he advised a brash newbie to be more circumspect when approaching his prey. As said newbie explained, after just having fruitlessly offered his services to two elderly white women out for a stroll after breakfast, why marry an equally poor Gambian woman and live out his life in misery? Indeed so: give me a white woman or give me death, although I did later meet an equally young man who had indeed married a white woman who shipped him out to Germany. He lasted just two years as a 'sex slave' (his words) before returning home. But who is anybody to judge, especially from the comforts of the developed world to which the inhabitants of the underdeveloped aspire?

The documentary maker who made the YouTube video, a youngish black Londoner, was himself mistaken for a local and was grabbed accordingly by white grandmas whenever he hovered around one of the many night spots; he used the words 'seedy' and 'degrading' to describe the exchanges. It certainly looked that way. It happened on this, my latest visit, that I found myself walking towards one of the tourist hotels behind a middle-aged British man and a young Gambian man who was pleading to be properly paid for his 'services'. You could see that the former was worried about possible violence as he quickened his steps along the short, narrow street of bars, cafés and bureaux de change, and it was with relief that he entered the lobby of his hotel to be welcomed by two male staff who quickly rounded on their compatriot. The humiliation for a Gambian of either sex with any sensibility by this modern version of a demeaning exchange between white and black, European and African, going back uncountable centuries with no apparent end in sight, is understandable. I daresay it accounted in part for my own experience with the young woman receptionist at my downtown hotel (800 dalasis/£8.48, as opposed to ten times that for the tourist ones), who was quick to see me in that light, and with good reason.

The fault was mine. I arrived late in the evening after an exhausting bus ride from Bissau, having crossed two borders (including the one referred to earlier where I snatched my passport from the immigration officer's hand), and snapped at the sleepy young man who was reluctant to carry my rucksack to the second-floor room I had been allocated. The receptionist, an equally young woman wearing a hijab, frowned at this elderly white man throwing his weight around, my Nigerian passport notwithstanding. Indeed, she probably thought my supposed nationality ill-gotten given the country's reputation for corruption even within the subregion; after all, even Nigerian immigration officials regarded me sceptically. It happened that I needed to renew my passport soon after this trip and was told to present proof of who I claimed to be despite my thirty-year record in their own files. The officer had the good grace to apologise for the inconvenience—she evidently appreciated that it was unpleasant to have your paternity doubted—but said that there had been an uptick in false claims by foreigners wanting a passport most indigenes would (and do) happily ditch for almost any other, ranking as it does below those of all the other countries in the subregion, and only just ahead of South Sudan and North Korea.

For the five days that I lodged at the hotel, the receptionist did her best to show her disapproval of me. For instance, she never greeted me whenever I came or went, just frowned and looked away, thereby undermining my position in the scheme of things. Halfway into hostilities, I asked her to help collect a bottle of beer I had put in the kitchen fridge. She said that it was against her Islamic religion to touch it and turned on her heels. On my penultimate day, I went in search of the light blue rucksack I had given the young man to spread after I washed it—the first time in over a month on the road—and came across her watching television in the communal lounge. She brushed off my question without even looking at me. In a fit of pique unworthy of me, I switched off the television and then went out to the backyard, where I knew it would be all along. On my way out that evening, I paused in the lobby, greeted two middle-aged men I had seen on a previous occasion, and called her a 'stupid idiot', much to the dismay of one of the men, who told me to leave it. She insulted me right back but the next day she appeared contrite, graciously opening the fridge for me to retrieve the last of my beers which I didn't ask her to fetch. I drank it slowly in the outer porch and then started for the bus station for what would turn out to be a twenty-hour bus ride to Bamako, the capital of Mali deep in the Sahel proper where the majestic baobab tree reigns supreme. I hadn't gone a few yards when I turned back. By now thoroughly ashamed of myself, I went up to her and apologised. The men had evidently spoken to her. She returned my look and wished me a safe journey.

*

On that my first trip in the subregion, I couldn't have known how quickly events were about to move as we entered the end of history that turned out to simply presage a new chapter in a familiar enough narrative. Even before my report was published, Nelson Mandela was freed from prison after twenty-seven years as South Africa quickly democratised while Nigeria, which once gave scholarships to black South African children and was loud in denouncing the apartheid regime with 'ordinary mouth', continued to move backwards as the military entrenched itself ever more deeply in power. This was the same military which burned down Fẹlá Kúti's house for calling them 'animals in human skin' for the way they treated the 'bloody civilians' they whipped in the streets. For my own part, our pariah status suited me well enough in my work with *Index on Censorship* for purely self-interested reasons. It meant I could spend more time in Lagos, where I was involved in a series of court cases to eject tenants from a property left me by my father, our fractious relationship notwithstanding.

I should also say that I had been irritated by the amount of space the magazine had previously given the then pariah apartheid South Africa—in keeping with the 'Western' press generally—merely because white, i.e. European, people were involved in a system they codified into law, even though equally brutal regimes were to be found almost everywhere else on the continent, their own supposedly more liberal laws notwithstanding. As Fẹlá put it in his always uncompromising manner, Mandela wouldn't have survived half as long in a Nigerian prison, let alone walk out looking hale and hearty. Indeed, had he been in Nigeria he might very well have been executed by the court which tried him for treason—such was the fate of Ken Saro-Wiwa, the environmental activist and sometime writer. This followed a military tribunal in 1994 under the regime of the late General Sani Abacha, the infantry general of the dark glasses and promise to deal 'decisively' with any 'attempt to test our will', which had pronounced him guilty even before it began sitting—and from which there was no appeal.

I have written at length elsewhere about Saro-Wiwa, a divisive figure who also happened to come from one of the 350 or so minority ethnic groups who pay the price for not belonging to one of the Big Three which between them constitute two-thirds of the country's population. In his own case, he also happened to belong to the even more minority Ogoni—just two million—whose land contained part of the prized light crude that became the country's raison d'être following the oil price hike by the Arab producers as a result of Israel's victory in the Yom Kippur

THE ARMY THAT TRUMPETS THE DEMOCRATIC CALL

War, the Ramadan War, the October War, the 1973 Arab–Israeli War or the Fourth Arab–Israeli War (take your pick). But what was bad for Palestine was good for Nigeria—or at least those with their snouts in the trough—which continues to supply Israel with almost ten per cent of its crude oil needs even as the government condemns the ongoing genocide; in the words of Yusuf Tuggar, the foreign minister:

> There is no justification for the carnage that is going on in Gaza...the complete disregard for the proportionality of force that is being meted out on innocent civilians. This carnage is completely out of hand and totally unacceptable. There is no way to explain the double standards; it has to stop...[2]

Between 1973 and 2005, when we were newly into our supposedly recalibrated 'democracy', US$20 trillion of oil proceeds was stolen, of which US$29.9 billion went to just five individuals, in the process giving us pride of place amongst the most corrupt countries on earth. Indeed, the former colonial 'master' knows well enough, given that a great deal of the loot is stashed in its offshore havens when it isn't buying houses in London, à la the now imprisoned Ekweremadu convicted under the Modern Slavery Act earlier referred to, or sending two daughters to Roedean (reputedly the most expensive girls' boarding school in the UK), as did Saro-Wiwa, courtesy of the contracts he obtained from the same Abacha who killed him, having been former neighbours during the civil war in the late 1960s when they were thrusting young men on the make. Yes, it's horrendously complicated, but there we are; alas, Nigeria's journey is indeed a long and tortuous one.

The titles of the pieces I wrote in the 1990s give a good indication of the mood of the country. The first, 'Living in the last days', followed the annulment of the 1993 elections organised by General Ibrahim Babangida after eight years in power. He then stepped aside as his 'personal sacrifice to the nation' in order to hand over to an interim government headed by a lacklustre businessman with no previous political experience. The fellow lasted just three months before he, in turn, was overthrown by General Sani Abacha, Saro-Wiwa's nemesis and Babangida's former deputy whom he had failed to retire along with the other top brass in order that he might take his own prearranged seat in the saddle. Meanwhile, Chief Moshood Abíọ́lá, the presumed winner and a businessman without previous political experience, quickly proved himself equally unfit for the great honour of serving his country by 'fleeing' abroad through the international airport in Lagos at the first sign of trouble and only returning after it was too late to exploit his popular mandate. His explanation at the time was his fear of assassination and his reluctance to split the country 'for the sake of my personal ambition,' to which end he eventually agreed a photo opportunity with the new pretender in uniform.

Abíọ́lá, the chief of 150 titles and almost as many wives, had obviously missed the dramatic scene three years earlier of Boris Yeltsin facing down a tank in Moscow when the would-be Russian president was called upon to fulfil *his* patriotic duty. Russia, unlike Nigeria, was clearly worth dying for, except that die he did anyway when, for a reason nobody can still fathom, he suddenly changed his mind on the first anniversary of his presumed mandate and announced at a rally in Lagos that he was, after all, President and Commander-in-Chief of the Armed Forces, Federal Republic of Nigeria. He died in prison five years later. Two years into his imprisonment, one of his wives, Alhaja Kudirat Abíọ́lá, an outspoken defender of her husband's presumed mandate, was machine-gunned to death in her car at a busy Lagos junction at nine in the morning.

More disheartening still was the long list of erstwhile democrats and would-be 'radicals' who saw fit to serve under yet another dictator on the grounds that the new administration 'is friendly and sympathetic to our cause'. They included Ambassador Babagana Kingibe (how we love our titles), Abíọ́lá's erstwhile running mate; Chief Alex Ibru, publisher of *The Guardian*, the country's leading independent newspaper; and Dr Olú Onàgorúwà, a renowned constitutional lawyer with previously impeccable human rights credentials. Why they imagined that any military government could possibly be 'sympathetic' to the cause of freedom was not a question that appeared to trouble them; worse yet, all of them knew well enough that the opposite was the case, as they were soon to discover: Ibru was shot in his car, survived but lost an eye and two fingers; and Onàgorúwà's son was shot and killed in the driveway of his father's house, which caused the latter to suffer a stroke from which he never recovered.

But then Babangida himself had also assumed power in 1986 on a pro-human rights platform but before his first year was out had reverted to type by closing newspaper houses, imprisoning professors and generally carrying on as though the country was his personal fiefdom. This last was made concrete by the Central Bank of Nigeria Decree No. 24 of 1991, which empowered him to 'direct' the bank 'as to the monetary and banking policy pursued or intended to be pursued,' and which, according to the World Bank, led to 'a breakdown in fiscal and monetary discipline'. A subsequent panel in 1994 reported that US$12.4bn accruing from oil sales, including the temporary windfall from the 1990 Gulf crisis, were unaccounted for. All that money went through special dedicated accounts, 'by-passing budgetary mechanisms of expenditure authorization and control', some of which went on seventy six-door Mercedes-Benz limousines for visiting heads of state when Nigeria hosted the 1991 Organisation of African Unity jamboree. Abacha continued in this vein, stealing up to US$5bn in his five-year reign.

And then, finally, there was the culpability of 'ordinary' Nigerians themselves. Barely three years after the annulment, they obligingly trooped off to designated centres on successive Saturdays to vote in local council elections in yet another transition to civil rule. The entire programme itself was scheduled to culminate two years later, whereupon Abacha would apparently hand over to an elected civilian president and the 'giant of Africa' would once more assume its honoured place among the comity of nations. Even more absurd, the 1994 elections themselves were held on a 'zero-party basis', ostensibly in recognition of the country's 'historical and cultural peculiarities' but, in reality, to enable the government to interfere at will without raising charges of political favouritism. In one state alone (out of thirty-six), one hundred prospective delegates previously cleared by the National Electoral Commission were summarily banned after 'further screening carried out by the state security agents' on the very morning that voting was to take place. The government naturally denied that it was intent on packing the councils with its surrogates but any debate about the matter was in any case academic. Section 45 of the Local Government Decree 6 of 1996 empowered the head of state to remove any councillor 'found to be compromising his non-partisan political standing', a piece of gobbledygook which could only mean what the head of state wanted it to mean. Additionally, Section 12 of the same decree ousted the jurisdiction of the courts in all matters relating to the elections. The head of state giveth and the head of state taketh away.

The government, of course, was delighted with the 'massive turnout', as the respected (and previously banned) *Guardian* newspaper put it, and a jubilant Dr Walter Ofonagoro, the information and culture minister, spoke the truth for once when he declared that 'Abacha's regime had been vindicated' by this show of numbers, estimated at up to twenty-four million. Imported observers from the United States whom nobody but the government had ever heard of, but who were nevertheless privileged to observe the sad spectacle from the air-conditioned comfort of their chauffeur-driven limousines (who said that Nigeria was a poor country?), promised to relay the good news to President Bill Clinton in order that he might stop once and for all any further talk of sanctions and freezing the assets of military officers. According to the statement issued by their spokesperson, 'I saw the eagerness of the people to vote... I think they should be encouraged.'[3]

Some sections of the Nigerian intelligentsia, for their part, revealed once again their limitless capacity for self-delusion when the facts on the ground refused to conform to their sentimental pretences concerning the behaviour of their wayward compatriots. An editorial in *ThisDay*, another respected newspaper of otherwise impeccable liberal credentials, contrived to interpret the entire charade as a 'vote for democracy': 'The message in the large turnout was clear and unmistaken: that the people of Nigeria are ready for democracy'; and the reverend Matthew Kukah of the Catholic Secretariat (the administrative headquarters of the Catholic Bishops' Conference), who was never out of the limelight pronouncing on every twist and turn in the nation's farcical politics (and who still does, alas), substituted emotive language for reasoned argument in his determination to prove that two plus two came to anything but four. According to him, the 'real issue' was that Nigerians 'are ready to come out at the sound of any voice that trumpets the democratic call,' which was why, 'hungry, thirsty, fed up, humiliated,' they were nonetheless 'still determined to assert their democratic rights for what they are worth'.[4]

As fantasies go, this was as dangerous as the notion that the military was capable of midwifing democracy (to use its own terminology) even as it continued to incarcerate journalists and human rights activists whose only crime was to call for the realisation of that democracy in the shortest possible time; but why a people ostensibly yearning to be free didn't simply use their most effective weapon and stay at home in protest was understood clearly enough by the aspiring politicians jostling for their share of the 'national cake' baked in the watery landscape of the Niger delta that had claimed Saro-Wiwa's life. Completely devoid as they were of any notion of patriotism and understanding only too well which way 'our people' would jump when the military cracked the whip, the would-be guardians of civil rule simply gave their compatriots what they knew they wanted: 'The amount is ₦200 [£1.50],' said one voter, gleefully showing his wad of banknotes. 'During the last election I did not get any money, but this time I must get something. I am here with my wife, my sister-in-law and her two friends. Between us we are going to get ₦1,000 today.'

This particular voter and his retinue were fortunate to live in Lagos. Five naira was apparently sufficient in some parts of the country to get the 'hungry, thirsty, fed up, traumatised, humiliated' to sell their birthright, but what to do? Any self-avowed democrat was bound to respect the collective will of the Nigerian people and never mind how deplorable one found that will to be. The fact that the Nigerian people themselves voluntarily acceded to the annulment of the 1993 elections, and any hope of the 'enduring democracy' that the Abacha regime never tired of promising to deliver even as it did everything to ensure that no such beast would emerge in the near future, only suggested a shabby collusion between the rulers and the ruled that could hardly be gainsaid by the wishful thinking of those who yearned for the giant of Africa to assume its honoured place, etc.

In fact, democracy of sorts did return on the eve of the new millennium, in part because the military itself was only too aware of its increasingly shabby reputation that only profited the minority 'political class' within its ranks that saw senior officers

THE ARMY THAT TRUMPETS THE DEMOCRATIC CALL

trembling before their juniors who happened to be, say, the military governor of a state. Handily, both General Abacha and Chief Abíọ́lá died in mysterious circumstances within one month of each other: the former at the hands of two Indian prostitutes flown in for that purpose (although the Indian high commission was quick to deny it); the latter just days before his expected release from prison in July 1998. He'd been held by the military regime for more than four years. The way was then left open for the military to organise elections which installed their chosen candidate, the retired General Olúṣẹ́gun Ọbásanjọ́ and himself a former military head of state from 1976 to 1979. But then Nigeria was designed as a semi-militarised state by the British colonial power which amalgamated one of the most diverse countries in the world—if not *the* most diverse—and which is only held together by sheer force, as proved by the first civil war of the late 1960s and the second that is almost upon us.

6

THE MOST SAVAGE ACTS

In the midst of all the Nigerian drama, and still on the staff of *Index on Censorship*, I undertook a number of trips within the subregion. One was back to Liberia in 1995, which I had left just one month before Charles Taylor's 1989 invasion that swiftly engulfed the country but for Monrovia, which was quickly secured by ECOMOG, a four-thousand-strong regional peacekeeping force convened by ECOWAS. I went first to my old hotel in the downtown area, but it was now occupied by squatters, refugees in their own country with nothing to do all day but sit on the balcony and watch the money changers on Broad Street, or venture downstairs in search of food. I was later told that the Lebanese proprietor had fled back home just before Taylor launched a futile attempt to dislodge the foreign troops and declare himself president, such was the scale of his ambition. The ensuing carnage, in which children as young as eight were recruited to join battle with trained soldiers, lasted for weeks and killed a quarter of the city's population. The traumatic consequences of these events were still keenly felt six years later during my second visit.

I was told a story concerning one of these children, a girl of ten or thereabouts. Ironically, the story involved another Lebanese man by the name of Ghassan. I had already heard about Ghassan from John, a tall, slight man in his mid-twenties who cleaned my room and fetched water and took me along to the basketball matches that were the only fun to be had before the evening curfew. It seems that Ghassan had once saved his life. It happened that one afternoon during a lull in the 1989 Taylor assault John went in search of food in Monrovia. On his way back, and already within sight of the building he and the others were occupying, he was accosted by a government soldier who asked him what tribe he was from, which was the standard question. John evidently gave the wrong answer. The soldier told him to strip to his underpants—just as Israeli soldiers are doing to Palestinians in Gaza as I write—and follow him. 'By this time, all the women were crying,' John said, whereupon Ghassan came forward and pleaded with the soldier. He said that John was his son and offered him fifty Liberian dollars (US$1) in one-dollar coins, which was all the money he had. 'If not for him,' John said and shook his head.

But it was another person, a young woman called Phoebe, who told me about the ten-year-old girl soldier. It went like this. One day, Phoebe and Ghassan went in search of food when a rebel jeep pulled up beside them, whereupon one of the rebels confronted Ghassan and said that he was going to kill him and drink his blood. Ghassan begged and begged but the rebel remained unmoved. Ghassan started crying as he entered the jeep but, as they were about to take off, Phoebe, even now not understanding what possessed her but knowing full well the possible consequences of what she was about to do, asked the rebel if she could come along. He shrugged so she got in. That was when she saw another girl in the front seat with an AK47 across her lap. They drove some distance from the city centre, the rebel all the while telling Ghassan that he was going to kill him and drink his blood. Finally, they came to a stop. The rebel told Ghassan to get down. Ghassan started pleading all over again and it was then that the girl in the front made her move. She climbed out of the jeep as leisurely as you please, stood directly in front of the rebel and calmly told him to leave the white man alone. The rebel refused. He insisted that he was going to kill the white man and drink his blood; that he had never before tasted the blood of a white. The girl soldier cocked her AK47, pointed it at his chest and said that she would shoot him if he didn't obey.

Phoebe paused for a moment, searching for the words that would properly convey the surreal nature of what she had witnessed, but then shook her head. 'And he obeyed her,' was all she could add. The rebel stood to attention, saluted the girl, and got back in the jeep. Shortly afterwards, Ghassan followed his compatriots back to Beirut. Before I left Monrovia on that my second trip in 1995, I asked Phoebe if she had seen the girl since. She said that she hadn't, although she was always on the lookout for her. The girl would be a grown woman by now, if she was still alive; and I wondered at the bitter harvest for a country in which children had learned to kill or be killed: one month after I left, unidentified militiamen attacked the small town of Yosi in the interior, which was ostensibly under the control of Charles Taylor's National Patriotic Front of Liberia (NPFL), and hacked sixty-two people to death. Although they were apparently armed with guns, the militiamen (or soldiers or rebels or bandits or whatever they called themselves) preferred to use machetes and clubs. Most of the victims were women and children, but then most of the victims usually are in wars of this kind, as witness Gaza today.

Everybody in Monrovia had their own story. There was AB, for instance, not yet twenty but already building a small house for himself and his widowed mother on the plot he had acquired. I called him 'the philosopher' because he was forever trying to engage me in lectures (his word) about the meaning of life. He recounted to me on more than one occasion how his best friend was beheaded right in front of him. 'Did you know that a head does bounce like a football?' he kept repeating in renewed astonishment. He might well have wondered about the meaning of life.

As for Samuel Doe, he was killed within the first year of the war on the orders of Yormie Johnson, Taylor's righthand man before they fell out. A former officer in the Liberian army and now a self-declared Field Marshal, Johnson made his peace with ECOMOG and helped in the defence of Monrovia but nonetheless had a reputation for casual murder. He was later held responsible for over 2,500 killings in the first two years, the most of any of the warlords. In one notorious case, he orchestrated the murder of six Hare Krishna devotees who distributed food to starving people in the city. Their offence was to write him a letter begging him to stop his carnage.

Doe, for his part, who was largely holed up in the Executive Mansion getting high on whatever, refused to acknowledge that the game was up. He even turned down Nigeria's offer of political asylum but what happened next is unclear. It seems that General Quainoo, the head of ECOMOG, invited Doe for a meeting and assured him of his safety. Doe arrived during a change of guard duty from the well-armed and better equipped Nigerians (commanded, as it happens, by an old classmate of mine I still see regularly at our old boys' meetings but who, alas, is sworn to secrecy) to the weaker Gambian contingent. Doe was escorted to Quainoo's office, where he was formally welcomed; most of his contingent, who had been disarmed at the entrance, waited outside. Suddenly, Johnson and his heavily armed boys arrived and began methodically shooting them before storming

Quainoo's office. Hearing the gunshots, Doe expressed concern but was assured that all was well. Quainoo and his aide excused themselves, ostensibly to check on what was happening outside, but never returned. Meanwhile, ECOMOG troops appear to have withdrawn, giving rise to the suspicion that they were in on it; had, indeed, initiated it to get rid of the stubborn Doe who refused to 'hear word'. Johnson's men moved indoors, finished off Doe's remaining team, and then shot him in both legs before dragging him off to Johnson's base, where his gruesome death was recorded for the world to see (and which can be viewed on YouTube if you are so inclined).

The YouTube video opens with Field Marshal Johnson sitting at a table across from Doe, who is trussed up on the bare concrete floor. To prove that he had no charms on him, he had been stripped to his underpants and the tattered remains of a five-star general's jacket. His arms are bound behind his back so that his elbows are almost touching; his outstretched legs are tied at the ankles. Rebel soldiers are milling about, laughing and joking; Field Marshal Johnson, a string of grenades around his neck, carries out a fitful interrogation as he swigs on a Budweiser. 'Gentlemen, we are all one,' Doe implores with an attempted smile, whereupon Johnson bangs on the desk and orders one of his men to cut off Doe's ears. The camera jerks to show the deposed president held down by several men while one takes a knife first to his right ear, then to his left as Doe thrashes around, screaming in agony. In one version, Johnson appears to be eating part of a severed ear. 'What did you do with the Liberia people money?' Johnson persistently barks at Doe, who in turn persistently refuses to answer, doubtless to the relief of his wife and children in faraway England.

Cannibalism was a persistent feature of what became known as the first Liberian civil war, which lasted until the election of Charles Taylor as president in 1997. Some people assert that fighters were encouraged to carry out such practices by their ritual specialists, while others may have simply improvised behaviour in the belief that this would make them powerful. They often referred to the human heart using mechanical images, calling it 'the engine' or 'the main machine'. During the third battle of Monrovia in April 1996, for instance, one Liberian newspaper wrote: 'Our reporters on both sides saw fighters engaging in cannibalism and sorcery. In some instances, the fighters would kill and butcher the chest and extract the heart and later eat it.'[1] According to Tom Woewiyu, Taylor's former defence minister, there was a good deal of this going on: 'We saw a lot,' he said, describing his time as Taylor's right-hand man, 'including the formation of a group of cannibals called Top 20'. As for Johnson, he subsequently did what Doe refused to do and sought asylum in Nigeria in 1992, where he became a born-again Christian while he ran a bistro, having apparently reconciled with Doe's family. His 'dream' now was to set up the African Centre for Peace and Conflict Resolution and Children's Rehabilitation. I never went to see him while he was in Lagos but I did so after he returned to Liberia and I found myself in the country yet again in 2019, by which time he had become a senator and a preacher to boot—'I am the servant of God whom He took from the battlefield and cleansed with His Blood'—with his own church, the Chapel of Faith Ministries, which held its Sunday service in the main hall of a primary school.

I wasn't looking for an interview when I turned up at nine in the morning and knew in any case that he wasn't inclined to grant them, but I wanted to see him and hear him and sit in a congregation that still believed in miracles. If I was lucky, I might even see one given that miracles are said to be his stock-in-trade. The hall itself, which could seat 160, was only half-full, mainly women and children in their Sunday best, some of whom smiled shyly at me but otherwise kept their distance. As I waited for the service to begin, I made a few discreet notes and presently looked up to see Prince Johnson himself striding purposefully towards me. He wore a light grey silk suit and pale pink tie, a matching handkerchief in his breast pocket. He was shorter than I had expected but bulkier and without the beard he had worn three decades earlier. He shook my hand firmly, looked intently at me through his steel-rimmed glasses and hurried away before I could speak. He was back an hour later for a brief, unremarkable sermon and took straight off before the end of the service. I lingered in the front yard for half an hour in the hope that I might catch sight of him again but without luck as some of the older men of the congregation huddled around a jeep occasionally glanced at me with amusement. Perhaps they thought—with good reason—that I was from some UN agency come to take notes and report back preparatory to finally charging him for his sins, but they needn't have worried on that score.

Incredibly, not a single Liberian warlord was ever tried—much less punished—for the wholesale slaughter of civilians they perpetrated, and this despite the recommendations of the country's Truth and Reconciliation Commission. In its final report in 2010, it described the now Senator Johnson as 'the most notorious' of the rebel commanders and recommended that he, along with Charles Taylor and 114 others, be tried for war crimes by a special criminal court; a further forty-nine were to be barred from public office for thirty years, while thirty-six were granted amnesty on the grounds that they 'co-operated with the TRC, admitted to the crimes committed, spoke truthfully and expressed remorse',[2] including the equally notorious General Butt Naked, of whom more presently. However, the government refused to set up a criminal court or implement any of the TRC's recommendations, which made it possible for Johnson to run for a second term in 2012, and this despite his mocking of the entire process by turning up at the hearings with much flurry and fanfare and proceeding to ridicule the commissioners.

This looked rash on the face of it but he had little to fear. Ellen Sirleaf, a Harvard-educated former World Bank staffer and Nobel Prize-winner, who was elected president in 2006 (thus becoming Africa's first elected woman leader), was also among those the TRC recommended banning from public office for her part in Liberia's tragedy. (It transpired, among other things, that she had given money to Taylor, whom she had worked alongside in President Doe's cabinet before they both fell out with their boss.) At any rate, she wasn't going to let the TRC get in the way of a possible second term in 2012 and dismissed out of hand its call for a special court—'Truth and reconciliation... has transformed into the Palava Hut...so I don't care what you say'[3]—Hillary Clinton having already described her as 'a very accomplished leader dedicated to the betterment of the Liberian people' midway through her first term. The UN Human Rights Council was still then muttering about imposing sanctions on Liberia if the government failed to implement the TRC's recommendations, but only the unelected permanent members of the Security Council were empowered to do that, so nobody took the threat seriously.

During her twelve-year presidency, Sirleaf mostly made the right noises about fighting 'public enemy number one'—i.e. corruption—but when asked by the local media why she had failed to sack twenty corrupt ministers, all she could say was: 'Because our system is like that... [Y]ou need to understand our culture, our values, our systems.'[4] During her second term, she appointed three of her sons to various positions. One of them, Charles Sirleaf, subsequently faced charges of economic sabotage, misuse of public money and criminal conspiracy following the alleged disappearance of more than US$100 million in newly minted Liberian banknotes during his tenure as a deputy governor of the central bank. When asked why she had appointed them, Sirleaf said it was because the country needed 'specialised skill'. It is to be noted, in this context, that in 2017 she was awarded the Mo Ibrahim Prize for excellence in leadership already alluded to because, as the citation notes, she 'took the helm of Liberia when it was completely destroyed by civil war and led a process of reconciliation that focused on building a nation and its democratic institutions,'[5] but then finding worthy candidates was always going to be a challenge, hence the number of years it wasn't awarded.

In 2018, she handed over the presidency to George Weah, a former striker for AC Milan, Chelsea and Manchester City, inter alia, and three times African Footballer of the Year. In round two of the elections, running against Sirleaf's vice president, Weah took more than sixty per cent of the vote. Whether he was fit for high office was anybody's guess, but the same was true of Doe, Taylor and—disappointingly—Ellen Sirleaf. In any case, people expressed their doubts quite openly. When I arrived in Monrovia one year into his presidency, preparations were underway for a demonstration by an umbrella group, Council of Patriots, to protest bad governance, corruption and economic hardship. There was some concern that the security forces might react with their usual heavy-handedness, but the protest went off peacefully. The EU, which ran a generous budget support programme, had warned that any government violence would be unacceptable.

The Reverend Johnson and his devoted congregation were happy with the idea that Weah could hold out for two terms when his first term ended in 2024. In one sermon, he proclaimed him 'our leader for twelve years' after he had received assurances from Weah's people that he would not be handed over to any court—national, regional or international. But he was also advised to zip his mouth, which was why he gave me the slip at the Sunday service; as he subsequently—and spuriously—attempted to justify: 'If we start bringing our past, our ugly past, as a nation, into the present, our future will be doomed,' having already been charged by the TRC of 'killing, extortion, massacre, destruction of property, force [sic] recruitment, assault, abduction, torture and force [sic] labor'.[6] As it turned out, Weah narrowly lost the 2023 election but then Johnson, who I was told was seriously ill when I attempted to visit his church on my recent trip for this book in 2023, died shortly thereafter and so—alleluia if you are a believer—must meet whatever justice exists in the afterlife.

Still very much alive, however, is Joshua Milton Blahyi, aka General Butt Naked, whom I also sought out. As his nickname implies, he and his men went into battle with only shoes and magic charms in the belief—paradoxically enough—that their lack of clothing somehow made them 'immune to bullets'. He himself claimed that he had received a vision from the devil telling him that he would become 'a great warrior and should practice human sacrifice and cannibalism to increase his power,' which was why, on capturing a town, '[t]hey bring me a living child that I slaughter and take the heart out to eat it'. Elsewhere, he stated how he would sometimes 'enter under the water where children were playing...grab one, carry him under the water and break his neck'.[7]

A garrulous man, he was the first to testify at the Truth and Reconciliation Commission that Johnson scorned, where he claimed that he and his rag-tag army of mostly children killed up to 20,000, or a tenth of the total in the first Liberian civil war, although few believe it was anywhere near that figure. Indeed, according to one Liberian expert on conflict resolution, he was merely seeking attention: 'It was a very sensational appearance. Out of the blue, you had Joshua Blahyi come in and make himself bigger than he was during the war. What he did was use the TRC to launch his career as a showman, as someone who wants to be famous—war famous.'⁸ Tellingly, he attended the TRC dressed all in white, and it was obvious at once that he saw it as just another pulpit for him to grab attention, having in the meantime started his own church, along with a rehabilitation centre on the outskirts of Monrovia, which was where I visited him.

I didn't expect to learn anything new, having already gone through the various documentaries about him, including *The Redemption of General Buck Naked* (2011), which was a take on his memoir, *The Redemption of an African Warlord*. In it, he talks about how he motivated the children he recruited by showing them Hollywood movies of action heroes getting killed and then a follow-up of the same hero having apparently risen from the dead. This made them 'more effective in battle' because 'everything they are doing is a kind of movie,' which seemed to sum up his image of himself acting out his own script to which everyone had to agree, including those he had damaged but now sought forgiveness from. There were three in particular. The first was a young woman whose brother he'd killed in her 'very before' (Nigerian parlance for in her presence). He accosted her with a film crew outside the building where she lived: 'I didn't want to kill your brother. That's war. I killed your brother out of madness.' Unsurprisingly, the mere sight of him causes her obvious distress. He makes a grab for her as she turns to enter the building, imploring her to consider him a substitute for the one he had taken from her. She is rightfully sickened by this obscene display in front of the cameras and the small crowd that has meanwhile gathered around but finally manages to break free. Unperturbed, he follows her inside and continues begging but she refuses before he regretfully gives up. His distress is palpable and all the more revolting for that.

The second is a young man, David Johnson, aka Senegalese, whom he recruited at the age of eleven and subsequently made his personal bodyguard. At one point, Senegalese temporarily abandoned his post at the so-called Butt Naked Barracks in Monrovia that was the warlord's HQ, thereby enabling a preacher of evidently much faith to accost Blahyi unawares. According to the preacher himself, he and his fellows originally prayed for all the warlords to lay down their arms in order that the country might have peace; but: 'God spoke to us specifically about Joshua. The Lord spoke to me that He could use that man. At the time, that place was a fearful place to go. But we took the risk because we believed we heard the voice of God.'

It seems he was right. Despite Blahyi's annoyance, he received them and even allowed them to pray over him, but as soon they left, he took it out on Senegalese who denied having abandoned his post and thereby letting them in. 'He lied to me, he lied to me,' he shouted, still incensed even now, and promptly shot him in both legs. He then dragged him into a bathroom, where he was left for a week—his colleagues must have been sneaking him in water and food behind Oga's back—before he was allowed to be taken to a hospital, by which time it was too late to save his legs. We first meet him in his wheelchair at a bus station, where he is begging for alms. Again, Blahyi seeks him out and begs his forgiveness. Senegalese at first refuses but then succumbs on the grounds that, 'he could have shot me in my body or my head,' and concludes, 'I think he loved me at that time,' while the man responsible for his condition takes him on a tour of the city for all to see. Alas, shortly afterwards Senegalese contracted TB and died when he was 'pushed out' of the hospital because he couldn't pay the bill. Blahyi, who wasn't in the country at the time, put on a sickening show of narcissistic remorse when he heard the news as he sought to make himself, as always, the centre of another's tragedy:

> I'm the one who caused him to lose his legs. And God made it possible that he was able to forgive me. And I came around and he accepted

me. I'm the only one that he looked forward to. I didn't have to give him but at last I was giving him a lot of hope. A lot of encouragement that things are going to be better. One day things are going to change.

The third person is a woman whose husband he killed 'in her before' and whose daughter, then a baby, he blinded in one eye when he lashed out with the butt of his gun. 'I don't want you to feel that I'm imposing myself,' he says to her when she finally agrees to meet him. She forgives him and even accepts an invitation to attend his church the following Sunday, whereupon he calls her and her daughter forward and regales the congregation with the story of what he did to them. She is uncomfortable with the unexpected spotlight because, as she says, nobody in the community knew her story and now everybody does, but Blahyi is not concerned with her, only the gullible congregation desperate for miracles in a world that offers them little else. As one of the more clear-eyed observers in the film put it: 'He's a selfish person. And he does everything with self-benefit attached to it.' Alas, all too many seemed to have been taken in by him. These included even the commissioners on the TRC, along with an evangelical white American woman who bought into the fable he recounts in his memoir that in his early childhood he was initiated into the dark arts—he subsisted on chalk, flew through the air and was anointed high priest of a secret society that required him to perform monthly human sacrifices—and took to sending him US$80 a month to help with his work.

I was surprised when even Joseph Nah Jlaka, my Liberian host who had endured the civil war in his early youth, and who had refused to accompany me to see Yormie Johnson on my previous visit to the country, had no objection to a meeting with Blahyi on the grounds that he had repented. As he put it in a subsequent text to me while I was working on this book:

> I don't support any warlords or criminal personnel or those waging wars for self-empowerment in wealth pretending to liberate people. They must all be brought to Justice. Butt Naked as he is called must also be brought to Justice despite he's always in the forgiveness when addressing forums or meeting people of all kinds, this shows that he's asking GOD for forgiveness. This is my reason why I listened to him in forums continually if there will be a change in his words. But for the other warlord, Prince [Yormie] Johnson, he's wicked and evil in all his speeches and boastful of killing and don't regret anything. So I don't like him nor listen to his speeches at all times, even in so-called church or radio stations.

For my own part, I have to say that the now forty-eight-year-old Blahyi cut an impressive figure as he sat on the porch of his Monrovia rehabilitation centre surrounded by the young men he needed for protection—he was fearful of being assassinated—as he played a game of checkers and spoke feelingly of the former child soldiers he was trying to help. Most of them were scorned by their families and had difficulty finding work. You came across them wandering aimlessly around Monrovia looking for scraps, which was why it was dangerous to be out on the streets alone at night—especially if you look like a white. As if on cue, one of them emerged from the back and stumbled uncertainly towards us, seemingly high on whatever. He finally came to rest against the interlocking fence that surrounded the immediate vicinity of the extensive bungalow for extra security. Blahyi regarded him thoughtfully for a few minutes, then shook his head in apparent sorrow and signalled for him to be escorted back. Given what I knew of the man, I didn't doubt—and don't doubt now, many months later—that this had been stage-managed purely for my benefit.

'I am responsible for what is happening to him,' he declared melodramatically, before reiterating that he was fully prepared to confess his many crimes before the International Criminal Court and take his punishment, but as we have seen—and as he well knows—this is unlikely to happen. Indeed, the only person to be hauled before the ICC and subsequently imprisoned was Charles Taylor, not for anything he did in Liberia but for his apparent role in the civil war in neighbouring Sierra Leone. It happened that he had been initially supported in his invasion of Liberia by the Revolutionary United Front (RUF), an aspiring insurgency in Sierra Leone under Foday Sankoh—with whom Taylor had trained in Libya—and which now wanted help in return. But he was also incensed by the fact that ECOMOG, having secured Monrovia in late 1990, was using Sierra Leone as a forward base and launchpad for operations in Liberia and vowed in a 1991 BBC interview that the country would 'taste the bitterness of war' as a result.[9] To that end, he helped train RUF fighters in the areas of Liberia he had 'liberated' and sent his own fighters alongside them into Sierra Leone. Indeed, it was calculated that Taylor's NPFL outnumbered Sankoh's RUF by four to one, so much so that it began to seem that the presence of the RUF was merely to lend an indigenous flavour to the incursions.

Taylor continued to fan what would turn out to be an eleven-year civil war in Sierra Leone (1991–2002) even after he finally secured the Liberian presidency in 1997 following an internationally brokered peace agreement. But he was back at war in his own country following a new insurgency two years later, by which time the RUF had captured the entire country but for Monrovia. Taylor's position eventually became untenable, and he was forced to step down in 2001 with the promise of asylum in Nigeria, which turned out to be a ruse designed to get him out of the Executive Mansion. Two years later, he was declared wanted by the ICC—the same body that at the time of writing has set its sights on Israel's prime minister, Benjamin Netanyahu, and Yoav Gallant, the defence minister—and arrested as he tried to flee from Nigeria. Taylor was initially taken to Sierra Leone, which had set up its own TRC under the authority of the ICC, but was subsequently transferred to The Hague on the grounds that his presence in Freetown for the duration of a lengthy trial might subvert the precarious internationally brokered peace struck in 2002. He was eventually convicted and sentenced to fifty years, which he is currently serving in the United Kingdom, although he never personally took part in the atrocities committed by either the RUF or his own 'special forces'.

As laid out in Sierra Leone's TRC report, *Witness to Truth*,[10] both rebels and government forces committed atrocities, but 'the RUF was the major belligerent group and dominates accounts of having committed the most savage acts against the civilian population'. It was particularly responsible 'for most of the acts of rape and sexual violence recorded,' especially after 1994, when it switched from conventional to guerrilla warfare. The numerous firsthand accounts make for horrific reading; the ones I reproduce here give an idea of the obscene levels of depravity visited upon the populace:

1. At Christmas time, I decided to spend it in the village of Konima since that was my husband's home. About morning time, the RUF attacked the village; I escaped, but they killed several people... An old blind woman was given cassava to eat; they (RUF rebels) caught her and beat her to death... Mariama Kalilu was a pregnant woman... When they met her in the room, they split her stomach open and abandoned her until she completely decomposed. They also caught one of my daughters who was a scholar and sexed her to death as she kept screaming until she was dead... Another suckling mother was shot dead and her baby kept playing with her remains for four days and by the time elders could decide to come back for the baby, she too was now dead. They were not buried but left for birds to help themselves...

2. We hid and left the town and reached a village called Fabu where we rested. We took the route to Senehun, a town on Bo highway, to get transport for Bo town. Upon reaching the town, we saw a crowd of people standing in a line: everyone was asked to dance. Sons-in-law were to dance with their mothers-in-law and sons with their mothers, so my son and I started dancing. The instruction was we should hold each other's private parts and ask it how it was doing. There was a song for this exercise. My son, being shocked and filled with shame, couldn't follow the instructions properly. I danced properly so that the rebels won't take notice of my son's stubbornness and kill him. However, after the dancing exercise my son was slaughtered right in front of me. They gave me his head, which I refused to hold. At this point I fled with other people and the rebels started shooting behind us, but as God could have it we managed to cross the river.

3. The captain of the RUF placed a bet with his colleague that the woman was having a baby girl whilst the colleague insisted that it was a boy. The pregnant woman's stomach was then dissected to prove who was right. After opening the pregnant woman's stomach, they saw a baby girl who was later left to die and the pregnant woman had already died from the act. This is one of the worst violations I have ever witnessed in life and when ever I think about it, I become more traumatised...

4. They were snatching babies and infants from their mother's arms and tossing them in the air. The babies would free fall to their deaths. At other times, they would also chop them from the back of their heads to kill them, you know like you do when you slaughter chickens... One time, we came across two pregnant women. They tied the women with their legs spread eagled and took a sharpened stick and jabbed them inside their wombs until the babies came out on the stick.

5. I was captured alone in the village by many rebels. They asked me to choose between death and amputation and I was unable to reply. They began to decide among themselves what to do to me. They finally agreed to cut off one of my feet. They brought a bulky stick and placed my foot on it; they first used a cutlass but it was blunt. They finally used an axe to amputate my right foot and went away...
6. They came back to me saying I should go and see what they were doing to my son...and they brought him to the field... and they cut my son to pieces alive. I was under gunpoint and all the soldiers were in uniforms... They cut my son to pieces with a knife and when they opened his chest, they took out his heart and cut a piece of it and pushed it into my mouth saying you must eat it... Then they cut off his head. They laid it in my hands saying 'go and breast feed your son' and they started dancing.
7. In the morning, we saw many rebels coming towards us... we were about to run but they said if you move, we will fire on you and they started firing all about... [T]hey came back to us and surrounded us. They stripped us naked...we were over twenty that were stripped naked. They instructed us to lie down on the ground. Then the civilian men who were amongst us were divided out, one man to a woman, until it came to a time that there was no other man for the remaining women who were lying on the ground. So after the distribution, they instructed the men to rape us. The women who were left without civilian men, they dug sticks into their vagina.
8. When we reached a forest-like area, I suspected from their action that they wanted to kill me or my child. So I kept my gaze on them. Not long after, one of the rebels forcefully took my child, held her on one of her arms and cut her open on her spinal cord. Before he could do this, I rushed to

hold his hand and when he turned around with his cutlass, he also cut me open on my head. He threw my then dead child in one corner whilst I laid in the other... Despite my condition that time, I stood up to collect my dead child. Again he turned around and saw me, he said to me that I was stubborn; he came back and told me to put my hand on a stump or else he would kill me there and then. I put out my hand, which he amputated with just one hit of his sharp cutlass. All the wrist bones were cut except the two sides of the wrist skin, which connected the amputated wrist with the rest of my hand.

As I write, the internet is full of the atrocities Israel's 'most moral army in the history of warfare' is visiting on the people of Gaza, but then the Palestinians are 'human animals', i.e. other, and so grown men can be raped to death in detention, for instance, for simply being men, i.e. 'terrorists', while children are executed by a single bullet to the head. Yet what is the excuse for African barbarity against their fellow Africans who are not 'other' but for a species of self-contempt, the legacy of a history we are failing to confront? The same history which continues to be visited on the continent by those who enslaved and colonised us, hence the outrage at Netanyahu and Gallant's arrest warrants by the ICC that was 'built for Africa and thugs like Putin,' as Karim Khan, the ICC prosecutor, was bluntly told by 'senior elected leaders' when he first suggested holding the Israeli leadership to account for what all the world but the 'West' believe is possible genocide.

All the world, that is, except Africa itself. With the honourable exception of South Africa, which the US is making pay the price, African governments have remained largely silent. Indeed, I was dismayed but not surprised at how little the plight of the Palestinians was discussed by the people I interacted with in the course of my journey. There was little if any outrage at what the world's most moral army was up to, not excepting the obscene videos that its own soldiers posted on social media that quickly went viral in the world's first televised genocide. As in the case with General Butt Naked, I turned to Joseph, my Liberian friend (and a staunch Christian, as it happens), for his take:

> I personally support Israel the right to defend itself from external attacks by any invaders or terrorists, or by that group calling itself Hamas. I feel deeply sorry for the loss of lives on both sides, including the heavy loss of lives from Palestine. But I end to say that Palestinians must distance themselves from Hamas and any other terrorist groups in order to have total peace in the region. The world needs peace, and peace must prevail for the children of GOD to live happily.

*

Today, Liberians still argue bitterly about Taylor's trial and the sentence handed down, but the real source of contention is not whether Taylor was or wasn't a war criminal but why he became a focus of international justice in the first place. The issue here is even-handedness. The court in Freetown was set up under the aegis of the ICC after a request to the UN Security Council from the Sierra Leonean government. But three permanent members—China, Russia and the US—are not party to the treaty that established the ICC, and there is scepticism not just in Liberia but across the continent as to why three major world powers should approve the prosecution of war crimes in Africa when they wouldn't dream of letting their own citizens go before any such court. There was also the awkward fact that the George W. Bush administration (in concert with Tony Blair's government in the UK) was at the time waging an even more devastating (and equally illegal) war on Iraq, also to unseat a president, and that a previous administration had supplied arms to the Libyan rebels to overthrow Colonel Gaddafi, Taylor's mentor. Fortunately for them, the 'international' NGOs were on hand to provide the moral imperative to justify this latest example of realpolitik that had seen only Africans indicted before Putin decided to invade Ukraine. One such, Human Rights Watch, even put out a short documentary detailing its efforts to help establish Sierra Leone's special court in the first place, and its subsequent success in convincing 'the entire' Security Council that Taylor's exile was 'only temporary', which they proved by making it 'clear' to the supine Nigerian president, Olúṣẹgun Ọbásanjọ́, that he would only meet with Bush while on a trip to Washington if Taylor was surrendered to justice.

That said, I quickly observed on this trip that Liberia has been rebuilt with impressive speed and the road networks are now even better than when I was last there. But the graft has gotten worse. On my eight-hour trip in a shared taxi from the Côte d'Ivoire border to Monrovia, we were stopped more than half a dozen times by Immigration and Customs and charged an informal fee each time. On one occasion, having refused to pay, I was singled out for a one-on-one interview by a 'chief' in the privacy of his office: 'a big man like you', he said, could surely 'find something'. We both laughed as I peeled off a few notes from the wad of local currency I had to cart around for this sort of occasion. Anyway, he explained, it was a security issue: no money, no surveillance, and no safety for travellers or foreign nationals. Didn't I know about the civil war that had raged in Liberia back in the day? I was later told by one of my fellow passengers that he and his colleagues hadn't been paid in months.

Monrovia itself has been reconstructed from the ruins of the conflict, but a second wave of post-civil war building, including a new National Assembly complex—courtesy of a China now positioning itself as the new imperial power in Africa, along with Russia, its junior partner by some distance—is the most striking. The downtown area, which was badly damaged during the war, is again as commercialised as it was thirty years ago, with street vendors crowding out the entrances to the shops, but the Lebanese-owned hotels, once popular with travellers and diplomats, are shuttered, along with their ground-floor restaurants where food was plentiful and cheap because Monrovia was—and remains—a freeport. Meanwhile, people are fearful of the precarious peace even as they look back with fondness to the relative stability of the Cold War years. My friend Joseph had lived through the war as a teenager and now spoke of Doe's reign as a welcome period of peace. I heard the same sentiment repeated by other people I ran into, including journalists like the editor of the *Daily Observer*, one of the two newspapers that had borne the brunt of Doe's fury. At the time, I was astonished by the energy and commitment of the journalists I met. Now it felt different. The paper can print whatever it likes, but the commitment has dwindled, along with the readership: everybody is getting all the news they could want from the internet. The editor, browsing on his screen as we talked, told me the paper was scraping by on government ads. His predecessors would have been scornful, but I was pleased, at any rate, to link up with Kenneth Best, the proprietor I remembered from all those years ago, a fiery man then in his early fifties whose contempt for Samuel Doe was all too evident even as he was reduced to selling bread while he waited for his paper to be allowed to open again.

Now in his mid-eighties, he told me that when the civil war started, he had fled to The Gambia, where he had established that country's first independent daily newspaper in 1992. Unfortunately, two years later he fell into trouble with the new military regime of Yahya Jammeh and was deported back to Liberia following a string of anti-government articles. He then applied for asylum in the US, where he had studied as a young man, finally returning home in 2005. I met him on the premises of his newspaper, where he squeezed my hand with surprising strength and laughed when I winced. It was evidently a party trick because he did the same again to both Joseph and me when we turned up at his house two days later at his invitation. A family member was celebrating their birthday. As I watched him beaming at everybody, I couldn't help thinking that he had survived everything that the long since dead Doe had thrown at him. That was indeed cause for celebration; as he himself said at the church service to mark his eightieth: 'Today, I want to thank Almighty God for bringing me and my family this far. I could never have achieved what my family has today without Him. He has been there for me and my family throughout.'

PART TWO

PART TWO

7

THE COLONISATION CONTINUATION PACT

So much for Anglophone West Africa but what of our Francophone brothers and sisters whose area at 1.8m square miles is four times larger, although almost half of it—Burkina Faso, Mali, Niger—borders the Sahara, which is why their combined population of 155 million is still less than Nigeria's alone. Ironically, France very nearly didn't have an African empire to begin with following the country's defeat in the 1871 Franco–Prussian War and Germany's subsequent annexation of the French province of Alsace-Lorraine. This initially caused France to abandon its colonial ambitions and withdraw its military garrisons from its West African trading posts, leaving them in the care of resident merchants. The trading post at Grand-Bassam was handed over to a shipper from Marseille, who in 1878 was named Resident of the Establishment of Ivory Coast. However, Germany's subsequent defeat in the First World War, and with it the loss of its colonial possessions to Britain and France (of which Togo was the only one in West Africa), was a gamechanger, as was the Second World War two decades later, which saw the rise of the US and the Soviet Union, both of which opposed the old imperial order for their own reasons, thereby giving added impetus to the burgeoning anti-colonial movements. But where Britain took a more laissez-faire attitude by creating 'a class [with] a vested interest in co-operation' that persists to this day (as in Lord Lugard's: 'I wish to try whether we can succeed in ruling the country through the Fulani [who] must be our puppets and adopt our methods and rules'[1]), France took no risks in its anxiety to maintain its global grip in a world where English had become the lingua franca; as the future president François Mitterrand said at the time: 'Without Africa, France will have no history in the twenty-first century'.[2]

The key was the so-called cooperation agreements that gave France continued control over the resources of the territories and were boldly acknowledged as such by Michel Debré, the French premier from 1958 to 1962: 'We grant independence on condition that the independent state endeavours to respect the cooperation agreements... The one does not go without the other.' In short, decolonisation 'did not mark the end, but rather a restructuring of the imperial relationship,'[3] and made more imperative by their concomitant defeats in Indochina, where the indigenes had a better sense of their history in their language, in Vietnam's case even later defeating the almighty US.

There were a number of components to the 'agreement'. First was the stupefying issue of the so-called colonial debt. This obliged the supposedly 'independent' countries—complete with their silly UN seats—to pay for the infrastructure supposedly built by France during the years of colonisation. Never mind that the labour was all but free and the infrastructure was largely to ship the particular country's resources to the France that continued to keep them subservient, a clear enough case of having your cake and eating it. Just how much has been—or perhaps is still being—paid has proved impossible to verify but there is a precedent. After the successful 1804 uprising in Haiti which abolished slavery (the first such country in the western hemisphere to do so), France, setting a precedent that the UK would presently follow, made the country pay compensation—or, again more accurately, reparations—to the expelled French slave traders for the loss of their 'property'. This amounted to the modern equivalent of $21bn that was finally settled a century-and-a-half later, and yet we wonder why Haiti is the poorest country in the western hemisphere.

Then there was the right of first refusal on the purchase of all natural resources, including those yet to be discovered (nothing like thinking ahead, if only we would do the same), along with French companies having the right of first refusal in the award of government contracts *irrespective* of whether better deals could be secured elsewhere. In Côte d'Ivoire, for instance, the jewel in the imperial crown, French companies were in control of water, electricity, telephone, transport, ports and major banks, along with commerce, construction and agriculture. Other components of the agreement included the right of France to deploy troops and intervene militarily to defend its interests, along with the obligation to make French the official language lest 'the people' from the bottom up actually start talking to each other, but most egregious of all—at least in purely economic terms—was the retention of the CFA franc imposed by France in the wake of the Second World War.

The CFA franc ensured a fixed exchange rate with the French franc (subsequently the euro), guaranteeing its unlimited convertibility, a requirement to deposit fifty per cent of the respective country's foreign exchange reserves in a special French Treasury operating account, and the principle of free capital transfer within the franc zone. In effect, this enabled France to pay for imports in its own currency, in the process saving on foreign currency in a world otherwise dominated by the US dollar. Additionally, French companies were able to repatriate their revenue without any foreign exchange risk. The French economy benefitted greatly from a trade surplus which provided it with reserves which could be used to pay for France's debts. For African leaders specifically, the arrangement meant they could more easily loot the treasury, which was actively encouraged by their French masters, who also guaranteed them their grip on power as long as they remained good boys, i.e. slaves.

The template for the new relationship was the former German colony of Cameroon in Central Africa on Nigeria's eastern border, which had been divided between Britain and France after the First World War, with the latter getting the lion's share. It was one of the first French colonies to be granted 'independence', in January 1960, with France leaving no doubt as to who would remain in charge. This was achieved by decimating all opposition in a decade-long war that was under-reported at the time and continues to remain largely stricken from history. Central to the story is Ruben Um Nyobé, the charismatic leader of the Union des Populations du Cameroun (UPC), who shared Sékou Touré's view that a post-colonial future dominated by Paris would be no better than colonialism itself: 'La colonisation,' Um Nyobé argued, 'c'est l'esclavage' ['it's slavery']. In 1948, he became secretary general of the UPC and spelled out its goals: 'suppression of the boundaries created in 1916 between the two Cameroons'; 'abandonment by France of the policy of assimilation'; and 'fixing of a time limit for trusteeship, after which Cameroon would achieve independence.'[4]

The UPC subsequently embellished its demands in a Common Proclamation, which France interpreted as a unilateral declaration of independence by communists. The party retrenched and formed an armed wing, the Cameroonian National Liberation Army, but Um Nyobé himself, who became known as 'the black Ho Chi Minh', was quickly captured and killed in 1958. To drive home the lesson, his corpse was tied to a vehicle and dragged to his village, where it was put on display. All existing photographs of him were destroyed, along with his writings and audio recordings of his speeches, and people were forbidden from mentioning his name. With the opposition destroyed, the country was granted independence 'to those who claimed the least,' after the elimination, 'politically and militarily, of those who demanded it with the most intransigence,' according to Pierre Messmer, the governor-general. Ahmadou Ahidjo, the first president, underscored the new reality:

> Let me state it loud and clear: The past is what it is. We are on our part determined to look toward the future... Let's refrain from throwing an armful of wood into a fire which is about to go out... We have forgotten. Why do they want us to remember again?[5]

Yet the resistance continued. The UPC still controlled most of the country. President De Gaulle dispatched three hundred French officers and five battalions of mostly African troops, some of whom had seen action in the ongoing war in Algeria, who launched an all-out war similar to present-day Gaza: aerial bombardment, villagisation (compulsory resettlement), harsh interrogations, disappeared prisoners, public executions. Perceived enemies in exile were also targeted. One of them, Félix-Roland Moumié, a follower of Um Nyobé, was poisoned in Geneva by the French secret services. It was estimated that in 1960 alone there were more than 21,000 dead. Little of this reached the outside world. French journalists who were permitted to enter under strict conditions were escorted on aerial reconnaissance trips to be told that burning villages were the result of long-standing 'tribal wars'. The insurgency lasted until 1971 when the last of the leaders, Ernest Ouandié, was publicly executed. The final picture shows him smiling on the way to the execution ground, where he refused the blindfold. The following year, a book by the Cameroonian novelist Mongo Beti, *Main basse sur le Cameroun*

[Rape of Cameroon], which detailed what became known as 'the hidden war', was published. The book was banned in France until 2015, when President François Hollande acknowledged what had happened and agreed to open the archives.

In time, even Ahidjo proved insufficiently malleable and was replaced in 1982 by the still-serving ninety-two-year-old Paul Biya, who spends his time between a hotel in that same Switzerland where Um Nyobé's colleague was assassinated and his estate in France. According to a 2018 assessment by the Organised Crime and Corruption Reporting Project, he has apparently spent at least 1,645 days in Geneva's Hotel Intercontinental, where the daily bill for his entourage 'adds up to around $40,000 per day': 'At that rate, the cost of all of the president's private trips...would add up to about $65 million since he came to power—and that's not counting food, entertainment and the rental of a private plane.'[6] Whatever our many Anglophone sins, at least we know where home is, if only we can cohere. Meanwhile, French civil servants and military personnel run the country on behalf of the colonial power that never went away.

In this, Cameroon is merely the most extreme of France's continuing possessions, but the lesson was not lost on the others. Indeed, only Sékou Touré of Guinea-Conakry famously opted out of the arrangement on the grounds that 'we prefer poverty in liberty than riches in slavery' and was duly punished for his temerity. The three thousand French civil servants who left the country took all their property and destroyed anything they couldn't move: schools, nurseries, public administration buildings, cars, books, medicines, tractors; horses and cows in the farms were killed; food in warehouses was burned or poisoned, all to send a clear message that failing to sign the agreement would reap the whirlwind. But then many if not most of that first generation were happy to go along with what Félix Houphouët-Boigny, the first president of Côte d'Ivoire, termed France-Afrique in 1955,

THE COLONISATION CONTINUATION PACT

which is to say even before independence. As he explained to Ghana's Kwame Nkrumah when the latter, fresh in power, urged all the colonies to unilaterally declare their independence:

> Your experience is rather impressive... But due to the human relationships between the French and the Africans, and because in the twentieth century, people have become interdependent, we considered that it would perhaps be more interesting to try a new and different experience than yours and unique in itself, one of a Franco-African community based on equality and fraternity.[7]

Houphouët-Boigny's delusional idea of equality was ridiculed by François-Xavier Verschave, the French academic, who came up with his own term, Françafrique, as in the title of his 1998 book, *La Françafrique: le plus long scandale de la République*, noting that the term sounded like 'France à fric' (a source of cash, fric being slang for 'cash'), and that,

> Over the course of four decades, hundreds of thousands of euros misappropriated from debt, aid, oil, cocoa...or drained through French importing monopolies, have financed French political-business networks (all of them offshoots of the main neo-Gaullist network), shareholders' dividends, the secret services' major operations and mercenary expeditions.

To quote Malcolm X in another but similar supremacist context, the likes of Houphouët-Boigny had been successfully 'taught to wear a mask of self-hate and doubt,' for instance Léopold Sédar Senghor, Senegal's first president and well-regarded poet of many honorary doctorates for whom the French language was transcendent, divine, celestial:

> I shall be asked: 'Why then do you write in French?' Because we are cultural half-castes; because, although we feel as Africans, we express ourselves as Frenchmen, because French is a language with a universal

vocation, because our message is addressed to the Frenchmen of France as well as to other men, because French is a language of 'graciousness and civility'... For I know what its resources are because I have tasted and digested and taught it, and it is a language of the gods... The French language is a mighty organ capable of all tones and of all effects, from the softest mildness to the fulgurations of the storm.[8]

Slavish in its abject subordination to the superior 'Western' civilisation that narrowly missed crowning him with a Nobel Prize, but frank in its expression that other, supposedly more 'radical' voices intent on a more 'universal' audience—as in, 'why should I write only for the [forty million] Yorùbá alone?' to quote Wọlé Ṣóyínká, the English-language Nigerian writer who did win the Nobel Prize—pretend to scorn even as they do the same. Worse yet, Senghor actively embraced his subordinate status in the wider scheme of things (and this despite his middle name: 'one who shall not be humiliated') by arguing against full independence more than a decade before the fact when he called for a federal structure in which each territory would govern its own internal affairs within a larger French confederation that would oversee foreign affairs, defence and development, which is to say everything of importance as deemed fit by the headmaster. This was despite his central role in Négritude, the literary movement among French-speaking African and Caribbean writers living in Paris from the 1930s to the 1950s, and which drew inspiration from the Harlem Renaissance, the cultural, social and artistic explosion in New York during the 1920s and 1930s. In similar fashion, Negritude sought to restore the dignity of the African after centuries of denigration, as exemplified in Senghor's famous poem, 'Black Woman', which challenged the notion that white women were the epitome of beauty, and Europe the epitome of civilisation to which Africa should aspire (the god-like nature of the French language notwithstanding), but which only

THE COLONISATION CONTINUATION PACT

underlined the confusion in his 'half-caste' soul, à la W.E.B. Du Bois's earlier quoted 'two warring ideals in one dark body':

> Naked woman, black woman
>   Clothed with your colour which is life, with your form which is beauty!
>   In your shadow I have grown up; the gentleness of your hands was laid over my eyes.
>   And now, high up on the sun-baked pass, at the heart of summer, at the heart of noon, I come upon you, my Promised Land,
>   And your beauty strikes me to the heart like the flash of an eagle...[9]

*

Other leaders, unable to bring themselves to sign the 'colonisation continuation pact' but noting what had happened to Sékou Touré, attempted to sit in the middle, but this is invariably a mistake given that sooner or later—but usually sooner—you will get run over, and so it happened. Sylvanus Olympio, the first president of Togo, one of the subregion's smallest countries, proposed to pay an annual debt to France for the 'benefits' of colonisation, which turned out to be forty per cent of the country's 1963 budget. He went ahead anyway and started printing Togo's own currency, only to be overthrown and killed by a squad of soldiers later that year led by Gnassingbé Eyadéma, an army sergeant and former French Foreign Legionnaire, who reportedly received a 'bounty' of US$612 from the local French embassy. The military handed over to a new president, but Eyadéma overthrew that one four years later and settled down to become what was then the longest-serving African head of state by the time he died in office in 2005, only to be succeeded by his son, Faure, who proceeded to manipulate the constitution to keep himself in power. The most recent example of this political chicanery was in 2019 when the National Assembly passed an amendment that included the reinstatement of the two-term limit for the president as demanded by the opposition but without the retroactive clause, thereby allowing him to remain in power until 2030, by which time he would have been 'on seat', as we say, for a quarter of a century.

8

PLEASE, I'M BEGGING YOU

I had frequently passed through Togo on my way by road from Nigeria to Ghana—a single day's journey—but only stayed on one occasion in the late 1990s in connection with a piece I was writing on the plight of people with disabilities in nine African countries and included Togo and Benin because they were easy to get to and I needed two French-speaking countries. It happened that it was my last assignment with *Index on Censorship* and easy enough to get funding—the Danes and the EU, in this case—to research the plight of 'black cripples', as someone in the office was overheard to remark. As with elsewhere in the world, about ten per cent of the population in my chosen countries suffers one of the five broad categories of disability—physical disability, blindness, deafness, intellectual impairment and mental illness—but one rarely saw them in public unless they were beggars. Most families keep them hidden away out of embarrassment. Then again, the mere fact of being a woman in many parts of Africa is itself a disability, most obviously in the practice of female genital mutilation. It is believed that up to 6,000 are forced to undergo this operation every day in the continent, usually under conditions that guarantee high death rates.

The pity of it is that women themselves are active in their own oppression, but then there is nothing new in the oppressed oppressing themselves, as in a 1997 UN report from Sierra Leone I quoted at the time:

> A powerful women's secret society practised genital mutilation on about 600 girls in a camp for displaced people and many have developed complications, according to aid workers. The Bondo Society promotes female genital mutilation or 'circumcision'. It carried out the operation on 9 January in Grafton Camp in the eastern suburbs of Freetown. Health workers say about one hundred girls, aged between eight and fifteen, were suffering severe complications. The practice involves the removal of the clitoris and is usually performed with unsterilised knives and no anaesthesia.[1]

According to one study, FGM, along with the child marriage that is legal in two-thirds of the countries covered here, account for roughly half the maternal mortality rate. So, for instance, the case I quoted from northern Nigeria about a thirteen-year-old girl married off to a fifty-six-year-old businessman who complained to a midwife that there was something wrong with her because he had difficulty penetrating her:

> On reaching Amina's room, the midwife found that the little girl was bewildered, terrified, writhing in pain and bleeding from what looked like third degree vaginal tear... With tears in her eyes, she pleaded with the nurse to take her away from that "wicked man" who, in her own words, "always pushed a hard stick into my private part".[2]

Many of the girls who do manage to become pregnant suffer permanent internal damage known as recto-vaginal fistula in which the wall between the vagina and the bladder and/or rectum is torn due to prolonged labour and lack of access to health care. Unable to bear children any longer and suffering from permanent leakage of urine and faeces through their vagina, they become a social embarrassment to those who have done this to them and are turned onto the streets to fend for themselves.

Few countries in the continent pay much attention to the plight of the disabled, although those which fought bitter liberation wars—Angola, Mozambique, South Africa, Zimbabwe—were better than most given the number of war veterans with a moral claim that could hardly be denied; but the organisations I spoke with in Togo confirmed the words of a delegate at the 1992 World Congress of Rehabilitation International held in Nairobi, Kenya to mark the end of the UN Decade of Disabled Persons: 'Countries of francophone Africa remain the least endowed in terms of structures, programmes, projects or services in favour of handicapped persons. They also remain the countries where policies and strategies of integrating handicapped persons have least impact or concrete results.'[3]

So far, I have generally avoided making direct comparisons between the Anglophone and Francophone countries covered here, and it is obscene in any language to be able to legally rape a fourteen-year-old girl already damaged by FGM. In fact, this is only possible in English-speaking Nigeria, where the age of 'consent' is eleven, and French-speaking Burkina Faso and Niger, where it is thirteen. Nigeria also happens to have the largest number of child brides in Africa (twenty million girls and women married as children), and the third largest burden of child brides globally after India and Bangladesh. In French-speaking Guinea-Conakry, she would have been eligible for rape at fifteen, and sixteen in Senegal and Togo, along with English-speaking Ghana and Portuguese-speaking Guinea-Bissau. Only in English-speaking Liberia and Sierra Leone, and French-speaking Benin, Côte d'Ivoire and Mali is eighteen the age of consent. Islam has much to do with it, given that Nigeria's northern Muslims have consistently used their dominance in the senate and the house of representatives to block the child's rights act that would make eighteen the age of consent. Burkina Faso and Niger in the Sahel are, of course, wholly Islamic, but then so is Mali, which makes it an outlier in this regard, along with The Gambia; Guinea-Conakry is eighty-five per cent Muslim.

And yet, whether predominantly Christian or Muslim—or more-or-less equally divided between both in a deadly embrace, as in Nigeria—there is a marked difference in vibes between Anglophone and Francophone. The former were far less touched by the European influence because there were no European settler communities, just colonial civil servants on rotation until independence, when they left for good. On this journey, I was surprised anew by the number of whites running businesses in the main shopping malls in Abidjan, for instance, which is inconceivable in Lagos with five times its population. The result is a culture which is more 'authentic', especially in Nigeria and Ghana, as reflected in their dress, cuisine, music and language, this last resulting in the creative use of the colonial imposition dubbed Pidgin, as in the title of this book: be alert; don't allow yourself to be duped; no do *mumu*.

As a general statement, life in the English-speaking countries is less formal, as indicated earlier, which played itself out at the various border posts, where officials at the one would almost plead for 'something for us', and the other demand a fixed, non-negotiable amount as their entitlement. At the risk of stretching a point, it also led to my overnight detention on that visit to Togo to investigate the plight of the disabled, the first and only time I have been officially detained in all my travels in the subregion. It happened that we had just reached the outskirts of Lomé when my shared taxi was flagged down at a police checkpoint. One of the officers asked for my ID. I handed him my Nigerian passport. He looked at it, nodded his head in a way that suggested he had discovered something significant and ordered me to come down. I was perplexed but didn't think there was any reason to worry. I knew there were periodic security alerts in Togo following Eyadéma père's refusal to vacate the throne after three decades at the helm. It was for this reason that journalists were regularly detained and their newspapers impounded.

'What is your profession?' he asked, leafing through my passport.

'Publisher,' I said, thinking this was the better option that still involved the written word.

'What is publisher?'

'Books,' I said, 'les livres.' I tried to find the right French words. 'Pour l'école,' I added hopefully.

He shook his head, dismissed my driver and pointed to a police van parked in the shade of a tree on the other side of the road.

'Enter,' he said, putting my passport in his pocket and turning his back on me.

The van was occupied by half-a-dozen riot policemen eating their lunch. A couple of them looked bemused as they indicated that I go to the back. I was a métis, after all, almost a white man, and therefore entitled to some comfort, unlike the assorted street hawkers they had rounded up in the course of a busy morning who were squatting on their haunches under the midday sun with their wares on trays before them: calculators, watches, leather belts, cigarettes, boiled eggs. Presently, the policemen finished eating, strapped on their smart blue helmets and piled out. The hawkers were directed to get in and off we went.

It was a short drive to the first police station. We were taken to the charge room and told to sit on the wooden benches that ran along two walls. To one side was a cell filled to capacity with some thirty young men, standing room only. Policemen wandered in and out pretending not to notice me, so I just stared out the window and affected nonchalance. In fact, I was pressed for time but there was nothing I could usefully say or do until I knew what was going on.

An hour passed. Other young men were ushered in until the room could hardly contain any more. By now my shirt was soaked from the heat. A little while later, I caught the sound of vehicles in the yard outside. One of the policemen told us to stand up and form a queue. The man at the front was instructed to bend over and reach between his legs with his right hand and grasp the outstretched left hand of the man behind him, who was to do the same with the man behind him and so on down the line. I stood at the back and refused to comply and the policemen didn't push it as they led all sixty or so of us to three parked vans, my fellow culprits shuffling awkwardly, much to the amusement of the onlookers.

We set off towards the city centre and soon reached the main boulevard that ran parallel with the Atlantic Ocean on our left. I noted a couple of hotels along the way that looked as if they might be reasonably priced. It hadn't yet occurred to me, as we pulled into the central police station, that I might be detained overnight, and I could almost taste my first cold beer of the day even as we were instructed to remove our shoes and drop our bags and file into an empty cell.

It was a big cell—it could have easily contained twice our number—but as soon as I saw the bucket in the far corner, I decided to refrain from eating or drinking for the duration of my stay. It took two hours for the bucket to fill up, and that was before we discovered that one of our fellows was suffering from diarrhoea. The police, for their part, ignored us until five o'clock, four hours after our arrival, when we were suddenly ordered to form three lines. The desk sergeant, a neat, handsome man in a freshly pressed uniform, began taking down our particulars in a ledger: name, address, nationality, profession. I was the last. Fortunately, his English was good.

'But where is your ID?' he asked, shuffling through the assorted documents in the drawer.

'I don't know,' I said, 'you people took it.'

He wrote something in the book.

'Your profession?'

'Publisher.'

He looked up.

'Books,' I said. There was a short silence as he paused over the appropriate column and then one of my fellow inmates said: 'Professeur.'

He closed the ledger.

'Perhaps now you can explain what I'm doing here,' I said, but he ostentatiously ignored me and went back to his desk in the far corner. I withdrew to the back.

A few minutes later, three policemen entered the station supporting a man in handcuffs.

'Oh my God, who is going to help me now? Who is going to help me now?' he wailed over and over. I could tell by his accent that he was Nigerian. One of the policemen shoved him into a chair.

'Oh my God, oh Jesus, who will help me, who will help me?'

'Shut up!' the desk sergeant barked, moving towards him.

'Oh my God, oh Jesus, I didn't know the money was counterfeit, please Jesus, help me, help me.'

One of the policemen fetched him a slap across the back of the head which almost toppled him, whereupon the man started screaming. This was the signal for the others to pile in. They beat him about the head and body, scrambling over each other in their haste, and then dragged him off the chair, across the concrete floor and through to the back, out of sight.

'These people are animals,' the man next to me said in English under his breath.

'You're Nigerian?'

He nodded. We fell to talking. He told me that he had been living in Lomé for the last two years, that he and his brother imported second-hand clothing from Germany and that he had been on his way to the docks that morning when he was arrested at a checkpoint because he had inadvertently forgotten his ID at home in his haste to collect a fresh consignment of goods newly arrived from Lagos waiting for him at the motor park. This was my first time meeting one of the Nigerian traders who dominate the markets in the entire region, and I was to meet many more during my travels; indeed, it was impossible to avoid them. Like him, they are mostly Igbos from the south-east who attempted to secede in the late 1960s, for which they endured a two-and-a-half-year civil war. Nigeria was supported by both the US and the then Soviet Union, and this at the height of the Cold War in which they were apparently sworn enemies, but then both had an interest in the post-colonial order in which everything changes but nonetheless stays the same. Following the civil war, and effectively excluded from politics at any meaningful national level—there has yet to be an Igbo head of state all these decades later, nor will there be one for as long as this warped version of the country exists—they turned to trading, accounting for most of the eighty per cent of goods that enter West Africa through Lagos and on to Onitsha, long since famous as the biggest market in the subregion. There was even a literary series—Onitsha Market Literature—named after it.

Meanwhile, according to my newfound friend here in our cell in Lomé, lack of papers was the main reason why people were detained, including most of our fellow inmates, almost all of whom were from that same Sahel to the north. They were used to being picked up at random, which was why they didn't appear particularly perturbed.

'They are very backward,' he said; 'they don't understand that they have rights.'

PLEASE, I'M BEGGING YOU

This seemed rich coming from a Nigerian, but I let it pass. I was pleased to have found an ally and thought he might turn out to be useful—he told me his brother had been with him when he was arrested and was even now working for his release.

'But I don't understand why they arrested me,' I said.

He shrugged. 'Money, what else?'

'So why haven't they asked me for any?'

'They want you to sweat first,' he replied. 'That's all it is, you know. They have to supplement their income. The government even encourages it because they can't pay them properly.'

'They've made a mistake this time,' I said, only half convincing myself. I wrote my London number on a scrap of paper.

'Ring this if you get out before me and tell the person who answers to get in touch with the BBC and Reuters. Her name is June.' I gave him 10,000 francs/£15, which was generous. Indeed, half that might even have been enough to spring me if only I played along. But there you are; sometimes one is stubborn for the sake of it.

By now it was getting dark. The desk sergeant asked if anybody wanted to buy bread from the woman hawker for whom this was on her regular beat while his colleague fetched water in plastic containers from the standing tap outside. We were obviously there for the night. I was thirsty but I wasn't about to risk drinking it.

Time dragged. It would have been nice to follow what was on the television, but the desk sergeant deliberately turned the set away from us and lowered the volume while he filled column after column in his ledgers. As soon as he finished with one he produced another from his drawer and started all over again. He used a red biro to draw the vertical lines with a ruler and a blue biro for writing horizontally, pausing occasionally to admire his handiwork. And all the while he pretended that we didn't exist.

By about nine o'clock, most of my fellow inmates were sound asleep on the bare floor. I made fitful conversation with my friend, whose main topic was Togo's irredeemable backwardness. Even so, he couldn't think of going home because Nigeria's economy was in even worse shape. That was why he had come here in the first place and why, despite the abuse of his rights, he would remain after his release.

Shortly after midnight, a van pulled into the yard outside and disgorged a man dressed only in a pair of khaki shorts. He was quickly followed by four policemen who pushed and punched him into the station and then set about beating him until we feared for his life. What was especially eerie was his complete silence. He never uttered a sound as he fell to the ground and was hauled up and fell down again. It was as if the beating was no more than he expected, deserved even, and the greater his compliance the better his chance of survival. He might as well have been a punching bag: certainly, that was how the police appeared to see him. By now the others were wide awake and we simply stood there watching, unable to say or do anything until, semi-conscious, he was dragged off in the same direction as the earlier man. One of my cellmates said something in French, perhaps an attempt at a joke, but nobody responded.

About an hour later, two young women of eighteen or thereabouts were ushered in. One was dressed in a mini-skirt and a halter top that showed much midriff. The other wore a cotton dress that emphasised the outline of her body. Both wore cheap high heels. The desk sergeant checked their IDs.

'From Ghana,' he said, as though this fact by itself was enough to incriminate them. Clearly, he didn't like Anglophones.

'So, this is how you girls come and practise your business in Togo,' he sneered. For a moment I thought he was going to slap them, and for a moment they thought so, too, and cringed, but instead he took the keys from the nail and opened the door of our cell.

'Get in,' he said.

They hesitated.

'Get in,' he repeated, and gave them a shove. Then he turned off the main light and stretched out on a bench.

Inside the cell, the women clung to the bars and studiously ignored the men behind them. They conversed in low voices, but self-consciously. They knew perfectly well that every man was looking at them, mentally undressing them, even weighing up their chances, as perhaps the desk sergeant was encouraging them to do. It didn't matter that they tried to keep still, as though to minimise the space they occupied. Their presence was enough; and then there were the clothes, worn for the very reason that was now working against them.

'What if they decide to rape them?' my friend whispered, indicating the other prisoners. In fact, a few of the rougher-looking men—the dock workers from the Sahel—attempted to engage the women in conversation, but too many of the others were awake for them to risk taking it any further, at least until they could be reasonably certain of getting away with it. As time went by and the others started falling asleep, the pushier men became more emboldened, but by then it was too late. The morning shift arrived with the first hint of dawn and the desk sergeant roused himself. One of the newcomers, a round man with a pleasant smile, sauntered over.

'Where is the white man?' he said. I stood up. He said something in French, but I shrugged to indicate that I didn't understand. He shook his head and turned away. The desk sergeant opened the cell door and ordered the women out. He couldn't resist the lecture, which went on for a good five minutes, after which he handed them each a broom and ordered them to sweep the station. He then turned his attention to us and barked an order. Everybody stood up and formed three lines, just like before. I sat where I was with my back to the wall. The smiling policeman looked at me and told me to join one of the lines. I jumped up and started shouting that they had detained me without so much as an explanation and that if they thought they were going to get away with it then they were badly mistaken and who the hell did they think they were, anyway? I was more upset than I'd realised; I was shaking with rage.

'Okay, okay, go and sit down,' the desk sergeant said with a placatory gesture, and then busied himself counting off the others on his ledger. He was the perfect bureaucrat, though I wondered whether he really believed some of us might have escaped while he slept.

As I had suspected, my Nigerian friend was eventually released at eight o'clock, along with a third of the others. I saw the money change hands but nobody had yet said anything to me. It was about an hour later that one of those left behind, ID-less and pot-less, asked me why I, too, didn't just pay the 5,000 francs and go.

'Why should I?' I retorted petulantly. After another two hours, hungry, thirsty and beginning to wonder whether my newfound friend hadn't absconded with my money, I was tempted to make a deal, but before I could cave in help arrived in the person of the British Honorary Consul, Togo being too insignificant in the scheme of things to warrant a proper consulate—let alone an embassy. I heard later that the BBC Africa Service in London had been less than helpful when contacted; Reuters, by contrast, sent their local correspondent but we missed one another by a matter of minutes.

The Honorary Consul—'Yes, just like the Graham Greene novel,' she confirmed—was waiting for me in the police chief's office. The police chief, a pleasant-looking man in his forties, shook my hand and pointed to a chair.

'What happened?' he asked.

'Why are you asking me?' I replied. 'I thought this was meant to be your station.'

'Perhaps you'd just better tell him the facts,' the Honorary Consul admonished. 'That's how we do things here.'

I bit my lip and did as I was told but stressed the fact that at no time did any of his officers explain why I was being held. I also mentioned the beatings I had witnessed and the two women who were locked in a cell with sixty men for three hours. When I finished my long story, he opened my passport and indicated my photograph.

'You see, Madam,' he began, 'if you look closely, you will notice that the photograph doesn't exactly cover the space for it. That is why my men were suspicious. They thought that it might be counterfeit. We tried to get in touch with the Nigerian embassy to clarify the matter but, unfortunately, we could not get an answer on the telephone.'

'Why should anybody want a dodgy Nigerian passport?' I asked, my sarcasm tempered by the suspicion that he was telling the truth. Nigerian missions abroad do little for their citizens, hence my detention. What they hadn't bargained on was my British connection.

'Chief,' I said, 'I have only one question to ask you. How long are you permitted to hold a person before charging them?'

'Forty-eight hours,' he said without hesitation.

'It's really a nice country,' the Honorary Consul said as we walked out of the station. She paused by her car. 'And what he said about the Nigerian embassy is true. I tried to get hold of them when I was told that you weren't travelling on your British passport but...' She shrugged. So, I was free, twenty-four hours later, to have my long-delayed beer.

At three o'clock the following afternoon, I happened to be walking past the central police station—Lomé is a very small city—when two young men beckoned to me from the yard. They were standing by a heap of dead leaves, one of them leaning on a broom. I recognised them at once.

'Are you still here?' I asked. They explained that they were only now about to be released, which meant that they had been detained for longer than the stipulated forty-eight hours. Not that they would be suing anybody. They had no money for food, which was why they were pleased to see me.

In January 1996, the year before my trip, an army officer, Captain Azote, was purportedly mistaken for a 'terrorist' and shot dead in Lomé. In fact, Captain Azote, who had been dismissed from the army in 1986 following an attempted coup but later reinstated, was a member of the Ligue Togolaise des droits de l'homme. In Togo, detention without trial was only the half of it as Eyadéma clung to power, as he was to do for the next six years before he eventually died at the age of sixty-nine in a US hospital for 'urgent' medical treatment unavailable in the country he purported to rule. Just under a decade earlier, Russia flew in two US surgeons to carry out President Boris Yeltsin's quintuple coronary artery bypass surgery—Eyadéma had merely suffered a heart attack—while their Russian counterparts looked on the better to learn from what 'many specialists' worldwide had considered inoperable.

The word 'deference' springs to mind when I reflect on the difference between Anglophone and Francophone. It was what gave me the confidence to elide the 'race' (properly colour) card that I was never offered in the former who weren't compelled to sign the sordid 'cooperation' agreements that made explicit their continuing servitude. Paradoxically, it also accounts for the depth of the current rebellion against the status quo led by the Alliance of Sahel States that is causing the otherwise proudly post-colonial French president, Emmanuel Macron, his serial meltdowns at the insolence of the enslaved who have forgotten their place in the 'Western' world order of universal human rights currently being visited upon Gaza; who, indeed, 'forgot to thank us' for colonising them in the first place. 'It doesn't matter, it will come with time. Ingratitude—I know this well—is a disease that cannot be transmitted to humans,' as he delicately put it at a meeting in Chad in January 2025. Contempt is equally a disease, which can be—indeed is—transmitted to humans.

*

The only other French-speaking country I had previously spent more than a few days in was Côte d'Ivoire, one of the two ECOWAS countries where I could get a visa on arrival with my British passport—the other was The Gambia on account of the sex trade—which was itself a marker of the country's subservience to the 'Western' narrative now being challenged by the youthful military regimes further north: Burkina Faso, Mali and Niger. As it happened to be a Saturday, the banks were shut but I needed to cash a traveller's cheque to buy a ticket to travel to Monrovia in neighbouring Liberia the following day. Someone suggested I try the Hôtel Ivoire, described by V.S. Naipaul, the Trinidadian writer and an early hero of mine already alluded to, as 'the extravagant, air-conditioned fairground of Abidjan. It was the place that people came of an evening to look at and walk in, down the long corridors, and the air-conditioning was so good that many people came dressed against the cold.'[4] It also had an ice-rink, the only hotel in the subregion to be so endowed in 1995 (and perhaps still today).

'Are you a resident,' the man behind the counter asked, looking at me doubtfully. I may have been a métis but I didn't look as if I belonged in such a swanky joint. I shook my head. 'Then I can't change it,' he said with finality. I knew he was just being obstreperous but before I could remonstrate with him my companion, a young man who was undeniably local, started pleading, 'Please, I'm begging you...' I quickly shut him up and demanded to see someone higher up, whereupon the clerk relented, but there was something in even this minor exchange—my companion's deference; the clerk's high-handedness—which somehow seemed peculiar to Francophones. Such an exchange would never have happened in Nigeria, say, or Ghana, or at least not in that cringing manner, the automatic assumption that a clerk in a fancy hotel was better than a street boy and could talk to him as he pleased.

The other thing that struck me was the state of the roads, which were better by far than any other I had seen in the subregion, along with the extensive, well-ordered plantations that were the backbone of the largest regional economy after Nigeria: the world's largest exporter of cocoa beans, third-largest of coffee and the continent's leading exporter of pineapples and palm oil. Not only was Côte d'Ivoire among the wealthier ECOWAS nations but also one of the most stable under what many perceived as President Houphouët-Boigny's benevolent rule. He was succeeded by Henri Konan Bédié, his chosen successor without a vote being cast, who was overwhelmingly re-elected in 1995, the country having become a multi-party democracy in the founding father's dying days following widespread demonstrations by civil servants unhappy with what they perceived of as high levels of corruption. Bédié immediately tightened his hold on power by jailing several hundred opposition supporters; he also stirred ethnic tensions by denying immigrants from the Sahelian countries—a large proportion of the country's population—access to administrative positions. He did this primarily to exclude Alassane Ouattara—a former prime minister under Houphouët-Boigny—from running in the 2000 election given that his father hailed from a Muslim royal family in Burkina Faso. He also excluded potential opponents from the army, whereupon a group of dissatisfied officers staged a coup in late 1999 under General Robert Guéï. Bédié fled into exile in France, the mother country to which all past presidents retire if they happen to leave office alive. Senghor spent the last years of his life with his French wife in Verson, near the city of Caen in Normandy, where he died in December 2001; his successor, Abdou Diouf, did the same after forty years on the throne.

A presidential election was held in October 2000 in which Guéï vied with Laurent Gbagbo, a former history professor who had been twice imprisoned in the early 1970s and again in the early 1990s—he lived in exile in France during much of the 1980s—as a result of his union activism. He had run unsuccessfully for president against Houphouët-Boigny at the start of multi-party politics in 1990 but instead won a seat in the National Assembly and was now trying his chances again. But the 2000 elections were marked by civil unrest, mainly from Ouattara's supporters in the north. Guéï claimed victory in the election but then it emerged that Gbagbo had actually won by a significant margin. Street protests forced Guéï to flee and Gbagbo finally realised his dream—but not for long. Less than two years later, there was a mutiny by demobilised troops while Gbagbo was away in Italy; and although government forces managed to secure Abidjan, the rebels took charge of the north with their headquarters in Bouaké and threatened to move against Abidjan again, whereupon France deployed its troops stationed there on the grounds that they were helping to protect their own citizens. Gbagbo, who immediately returned home, eventually signed an accord with the rebel leaders creating a 'government of national unity' but before the year was out the peace agreement collapsed because the rebels refused to disarm. Gbagbo ordered airstrikes against the rebels in Bouaké, during which nine French soldiers were killed. The French responded by destroying most Ivorian military aircraft, whereupon retaliatory riots against the French broke out in Abidjan.

Given the levels of unrest, which some likened to a civil war, peaceful elections in 2005 were considered impossible. A UN Security Council-endorsed African Union plan extended Gbagbo's term for a maximum of one year but this had to be extended for another year because the rebels were staunchly opposed to the possibility of a second Gbagbo term. Elections were finally held in late 2010 with preliminary results showing Ouattara ahead of Gbagbo, which he contested before the Constitutional Council, claiming massive fraud by rebels in the north. The Council, which consisted of Gbagbo's supporters, declared that he had won by a slender majority and he was duly inaugurated. Ouattara promptly organised an alternative inauguration, which led to fears of another bout of civil unrest as thousands fled the country. Numerous human rights violations were reported by both sides which left 3,000 dead in just five months. Gbagbo was captured by UN and French forces in a raid on his home and taken before the International Criminal Court but was acquitted and given a conditional release.

Bearing in mind the violence the country had endured for Ouattara to clinch the presidency, which he won again in 2015, he decided to run yet again in 2020 in violation of the two-term limit embedded in the country's 2000 constitution he had contested. He did this on the grounds that a series of constitutional amendments passed in 2016 had 'reset his term count to zero', a lesson not lost on Togo's Eyadéma fils three years later. He also admonished those who called for civil disobedience to stop their 'criminal acts…so that after the election this country may continue on its course of progress, which it has enjoyed over the last few years.' This failed to impress the opposition, which urged its followers to boycott the vote in elections marred by 'intimidation, violence and electoral malpractice.'[5] Ouattara went on to win by ninety-four per cent of the vote with a turnout of just over half the electorate, in effect following the same dangerous path as the Gbagbo he had ousted a decade earlier, although he was apparently 'hurt and devastated' by the waves of unrest, which he attributed to 'young people high on drugs and weaponised by the opposition'.[6] He also expressed disappointment at his party's 'failures in the area of training young activists, in spite of all the efforts undertaken over the past few years,' and vowed that he would '[hold] officials to account,' but didn't say how even as he betrayed his open contempt for the majority youth in keeping with African 'tradition'.[7] It is only a pity that said youth go along with the insults—in the interests of African tradition.

It was also a pity that the seventy-eight-year-old Ouattara, a former IMF Deputy Managing Director with a reputation for hard work, transparency and good governance (at least according to the IMF's own assessment), was supposed to be different. When I met him in Paris at the turn of the millennium, he was in the company of George Soros's staff just as the Open Society Initiative was extending significant support to the entrenchment of pluralism in the continent. Urbane and softly spoken, Ouattara publicly identified himself as one of the potential leaders of what many hoped would be a resurgent Africa. As he wrote in a 1999 pamphlet, 'An African renaissance is unfolding before our eyes. Most countries, through most of their independence years, have been ruled by autocratic leaders; autocratic because, whether enlightened or not, they stood above the law.'[8] Now he had joined their ranks, tarnishing a well-regarded premiership which saw the economy grow by a respectable eight per cent per annum and the reason why his compatriots had been happy to grant him a second term.

As he was a 'boy' of the 'West', international criticism of Ouattara's stolen election was muted, but a report by Human Rights Watch revealed widespread violence perpetrated in opposition strongholds by the security forces in league with local mercenaries. According to one eyewitness account:

I saw a group coming into the neighbourhood in two Gbakas [minivans], blue taxis, and scooters... They were armed with machetes, knives, and guns. I went out with what I could to defend my village. The neighbourhood youth started throwing stones, and there were so many of us that they fled. One of the government supporters couldn't escape in time, and he was beaten to death by our young people. In the town of Toumodi the attack lasted for hours, yet no police officer intervened.[9]

As expected, the African Union claimed that the vote had 'proceeded in a generally satisfactory manner,' but that was par for the course as other leaders in the continent paved the way for similar power-grabs; in the words of a human rights activist: 'the African Union is an organization that primarily represents the interests of the powerful. It is toothless and ineffective, and it repeatedly proves itself incapable of ensuring prosperity, security, and peace for all Africans.'[10] For its part, the European Union expressed 'deep concerns about the tensions, provocations and incitement to hatred that have prevailed and continue to persist in the country around this election,'[11] but President Macron himself chose to remain silent. 'France does not have to give lessons,' he remarked when asked why Ouattara's case should be considered different from that of President Alpha Condé in neighbouring Guinea-Conakry even as he noted that the latter 'organised a referendum and a change in the constitution just to keep himself in power. That's why I haven't yet sent him a congratulatory letter.'[12] But there are obvious reasons for Macron's double-standards. As both leaders know, he needs Ouattara in place to perform his own sleight of hand: guaranteeing French control of the colonial currency.

Ouattara has long been a staunch defender of the CFA franc, once claiming that the matter was best left to the 'experts'. Even as late as 2017, Macron insisted that the CFA franc was a 'non-issue' yet was quick to do an about-turn in late 2021 when he and Ouattara appeared together in Abidjan and unexpectedly announced that it would be replaced by a new currency, the eco. Macron, who, as already noted, prides himself on being the first French president born after decolonisation, claimed that he would 'engage France in a historic and ambitious reform of the cooperation between the West African Economic and Monetary Union and our country,' to which end, '[w]e are taking a big step to write a new page in our relationship with Africa.'[13] Ouattara, for his part, was less high-minded: 'Our countries are primarily agricultural, and we trade mostly with the EU. Our currency needs to be in line with our foreign trade. We decided to continue to peg our currency to the euro because it's in our interest to do so.'[14] Yet, as an economist (and therefore an 'expert'), Ouattara should have known that not a single CFA country is among the ten richest in Africa, and eleven of the fourteen are considered among the 'least developed' in the world by the UN.

The currency name change is not merely symbolic but is the name of the proposed common currency for the entire region as put forward at a meeting in Nigeria's capital just six months earlier, which was why the country's then president, Muhammadu Buhari, expressed his 'uneasy feeling' at being frozen out of their deliberations. 'It's a matter of concern,' he tweeted, 'that a people with whom we wish to go into a union are taking major steps without trusting us for discussion',[15] although the same Buhari had been lukewarm about any such single currency at that same June meeting, counselling patience over a hasty roll-out lest it damage his own interests in the foreign exchange markets. In the main, monetary union has been an obvious long-term goal but was recently once again scuppered by our present incumbent, Bólá Ahmed Tinúbú, who, after his election, proceeded to act as France's lackey in the Sahel that led to the disintegration of ECOWAS, as we shall shortly see. Indeed, the whole point of ECOWAS was to integrate the market that would be easily dominated by Nigeria to the exclusion of France itself. In this context, it was Ouattara's good fortune that he could rely on France to realise his personal ambition above the interests of his country, but then it was Macron's predecessor-but-one, Nicolas Sarkozy, who had deployed French troops to oust the stubborn Gbagbo in 2010, thereby guaranteeing Ouattara's first term and his continued enslavement to Massa. And yet, and yet...

9

DO OR DIE

The final leg of my journey took me a good way through the Sahel, which is to say Mali and Burkina Faso but not Niger, which was closed to traffic because of the continuing Islamic insurgency that France had been unable—or unwilling—to contain. There are two main outfits. One is the al-Qaeda-affiliated Jama'at Nasr al-Islam wal Muslimin, the result of the 2017 merger of four extremist groups. It is based in Mali but is active across much of the subregion. With up to 2,000 fighters, it aligns itself with the wider al-Qaeda jihadist ideology and seeks to build a Salafi-Islamist state in West Africa, which includes expelling all 'Western' influences; its leader, Iyad Ag Ghali, pledged the group's allegiance to, amongst others, the leader of the Taliban in Afghanistan. From 2017 to 2023, it was responsible for more than half of all violent events across the Sahel, which it carried out with roadside bombs, mortars, landmines and rockets paid for by ransoming captives, taxing the locals and smuggling weapons, along with extorting both drug and human traffickers, both parties taking advantage of the 'teeming' youths desperate enough about their lack of prospects to risk death crossing into a Europe that is equally desperate to keep them out. The group is reckoned to have clashed over 1,700 times with Burkina Faso's army, and about half that with Mali's. It also targets volunteer fighting groups, along with communities it considers sympathetic to the state. However, under Ghaly's leadership it has lately been promoting 'combat action against security forces, rather than attacks on the population,' which is in alignment with al-Qaeda's broader global push to brand itself as more moderate than its main rival in the region, the apparently more 'extremist' Islamic State in West Africa Province (ISWAP), but that may just be a matter of semantics, especially if you happen to be at their mercy.

Islamic State West Africa Province operates mainly in northeastern Nigeria and the southern Lake Chad Basin, along with the country's northern borders with Niger and Cameroon, although it has more recently extended its activities into southern Nigeria. It adheres to the 'extreme' (that word again) Salafi interpretation of Islam which views all who fail to adhere to its beliefs as apostates and infidels, which is also why it makes a point of targeting non-adherents, often promoting sectarian violence and indiscriminate executions. It rejects existing national borders—which is reasonable enough in itself, given how they came about—and opposes elected governments, which it seeks to remove through the same violence said 'elected' governments used to achieve their power in the first place. It originally developed as a faction of Boko Haram, which translates as 'Western education is forbidden' because it leads to 'Western Ways of Life', including 'the rights and privileges of women, the idea of homosexuality, lesbianism...rape of infants, multi-party democracy...drinking beer and alcohol and many other things that are opposed to Islamic civilisation.'[1]

Boko Haram itself was founded in 2002 by one Mohammed Yusuf following his theological studies in Medina. Described more as a rhetorician than a warrior, his calls for jihad were vague and adapted for the occasion but resonated widely, as evidenced by one eyewitness's description of his return to the city of Maiduguri in the far northeast of Nigeria following one of his brief periods in detention: 'People came all the way from Kaduna, Bauchi and Kano to welcome him. There was a long motorcade from the airport as thousands of his members trooped out to lead him to his house. He came back like a hero.'[2] The insurgency peaked between 2009 and 2015, with the loss of 12,000 lives—even announcing its 'capital' in Gwoza, Borno State in 2014, which lasted just seven months—before it affiliated with Islamic State the following year, rebranding as ISWAP. Abubakar Shekau was its first leader, but he only lasted a year before he was replaced. Its total membership is currently estimated at around 5,000. In large areas of north-eastern Nigeria, it operates as the de facto government, collecting taxes and generally extorting locals, as well as undertaking kidnap-for-ransom operations, such is the feeble reach of the country's security forces, and which makes travel in the region all but impossible, especially if you look like a foreigner. I last went there by road in 2019 to cover the then elections; even then our driver had to avoid certain areas, making the journey longer than it need have been. Now I wouldn't dream of doing so. Much the same would have been true of the northern parts of Mali and Burkina Faso, which was why I was able to touch Bamako and Ouagadougou but not Niamey, Niger's capital.

*

As earlier indicated, the Sahel is roughly two-thirds the size of the rest of ECOWAS combined, the reality of which was rendered stark as we headed east from Banjul on the Gambian coast to Bamako, Mali's capital. With just one exception, all my previous journeys between capitals—as in this one—hadn't taken more than a day. Badagry in Nigeria to Cotonou in Benin was just three hours by motorcycle taxi, although admittedly I was practically at the border to begin with, having previously taken all of six hours to traverse the thirty-six miles between my home in Surulere in downtown Lagos and The Point of No Return; but then the city-state, whose name means 'lakes' in Portuguese, is a byword for incessant traffic 'go-slows' in the absence of ferries that should otherwise transport the bulk of the population faster and cheaper but which, alas, is hostage to the 'Nigerian factor', i.e. that the good of the few must always supersede the good of the many. Again, from Cotonou I was in Lomé in neighbouring Togo by lunchtime, even allowing for my slow start and delays at the border crossing, which was also a problem entering Ghana on my way to Accra, although with the friendlier vibe that was the difference between Anglophone and Francophone already alluded to.

    It was fortunate that we left Accra for Abidjan at dawn because it turned out that the border with Côte d'Ivoire closed at 6 p.m. and we only just managed to scrape through, although part of the problem was the terrible state of the road for the last third of the journey, which was also the case on the way to Liberia, the only border I had to sleep at before heading to Monrovia, but then Côte d'Ivoire is the largest of the coastal states after Nigeria and I'm not sure I was put on the most straightforward route. Fortunately for my fellow travellers and me, we were met at the station by a local who generously offered us sleeping space in his house for the night, along with an equally generous salad. Monrovia itself wasn't far from the border but the roads for the most part were being reconstructed after their ruinous civil war, and we were lucky to arrive at dusk. I still had to find my way to Joseph's, the friend I had met on a previous trip and who had accompanied me on this trip to visit General Butt Naked, the flamboyant warlord who boasted of killing many more people than he did in order to remain the centre of attention.

Monrovia to Freetown is only 370 miles but proved challenging because I had to change vehicles twice in Sierra Leone itself, and this apart from security checkpoints in a country still recovering from a civil war that Nigeria helped to quell. The checkpoints were particularly onerous: where have you come from? Where are you going? Who do you know there? What is your profession? I couldn't see the point of them and, as usual, I was invariably singled out as they looked from my 'white' face to my Nigerian passport and back again, a puzzled smile of faint disbelief furrowing their brows. On the plus side, the roads were in surprisingly better shape, thanks, apparently, to the European Union, as proclaimed on the numerous billboards along the way, our benefactors never being shy of advertising their benevolence.

The Guinea side of the border on my way from Freetown to Conakry was possibly the worst of them all as the soldier barked 'deux mille' before I even opened my mouth and threw my passport back at me, barely even glancing at it; but I couldn't have anticipated the ordeal I was about to undergo crossing into Bissau, capital of the other Guinea, one of the few remaining former Portuguese colonies of a country that was the first of the European seafaring nations to trade along the 'slave coast', having established diplomatic ties in the thirteenth century with Benin—kingdom of the famous bronze figures looted in 1897 by the colonising English, proof of which is the crime scene that is the British Museum (just ask Greece). As usual, I took myself to the bus park at dawn to book a shared taxi, but it turned out that there wasn't much traffic between the two capitals. I was eventually introduced to an Arab-looking man with a twelve-seater mini-bus. It seemed I was his only customer, although he assured me that it would fill up in the course of the day and that he would give me a shout when they were ready. By four that afternoon, I still hadn't heard from him and the young man who had accompanied me—there was always a young man I quickly befriended at whichever hotel I happened to be staying in, who was himself pleased to be useful to the well-heeled traveller (at least by local standards) looking for directions—advised that we should go and get my money back. There was an alternative route he could show me in the morning, much to the chagrin of the transporter, who couldn't bring himself to look at me as he painfully refunded my money.

So it was that early the next morning we set off in the opposite direction, where, on the outskirts of the city, he booked me a shared taxi for the three-hour drive to Boké, the lucrative town where Chinese companies mined the bauxite that the country was famous for. The driver stopped at an intersection and pointed to the motorbikes crowded together that were the only sure route to my destination. It was early still, not long past noon, and I was supposedly closer to Bissau than Conakry, at least as the crow flies (110 miles to 170), but I wasn't a crow and I hadn't bargained on the route we would be taking, which was not only almost twice as long but mostly on footpaths through dense bush. I might have guessed by the way my driver prepared himself for the journey by calling first at his home in a nearby village to drop the CFA25,000/£30 I had paid him and change his clothes for the ordeal that he knew lay ahead.

For a little over an hour, we sped along the beginning of a new road under construction that would eventually link up with Bissau and we had to cope with the flying laterite from the trucks we kept overtaking, but then he abruptly turned onto a track in the bush to begin what would turn out to be a six-hour endurance test in which I eventually felt every one of my seventy years. Indeed, it was only looking back that I realised how right some of my friends were to be sceptical that I would actually complete the journey when I first told them of it. I heard it in the voice of Dulue Mbachu of *War Games* when I phoned from the Sierra Leone side of the Liberia border as I waited for the shared taxi to fill up; in 'The Poet' Uzor Maxim's reply to a WhatsApp message from Banjul that expressed surprise that I had made it so far; in my partner Juliet 'The Painter' Ezenwa's sigh of relief when I phoned her on my way to the guest house in Cotonou, where she had come to meet me at the end of the journey that we might cross back home to Nigeria together; and in Edmund (call me 'Eddie', and now an Ndabu/High Chief in his native Calabar), who later confessed that he was absolutely convinced I would turn back at some point out of sheer exhaustion.

Indeed, they all might have been proved right if I had known in advance what this part of the journey entailed now that I was stuck pillion, but there was nothing to be done. Do or die...or something like that. At one point, we needed to navigate a river about a mile across and it was a relief to dismount and stretch out for the half-hour it took the canoe to cross from the other side, but then it was back at it once again. This journey would have clearly been impossible during the rains, although we still came across swampy patches the driver skilfully manoeuvred until he eventually didn't, and the bike capsized. The second time I fell back over when I tried to stand up in my muddy trousers, so I took to disembarking and walking gingerly across whenever we approached what looked like another swampy patch, although it didn't always work out that way.

In the meantime, the short tropical dusk was approaching even as the bush on either side got denser, sometimes obliterating the track as we dodged overhead branches until we suddenly happened upon a village of mostly mud huts and lots of domestic animals right there in the middle of nowhere. The villagers themselves paid us no mind as they went about their chores, the women washing clothes by the river while children played as my driver tore through, anxious that we reach our destination before full darkness descended. By and by, we arrived at the border, an iron post across the path that had suddenly widened although we could have easily got around it on either side. To our left was a clearing with a small bungalow and two immigration officers sitting on a bench on the veranda with a trayful of loose cigarettes before them. Perhaps I was that day's only customer, but they quickly accepted the obligatory CFA10,000 and off we went, finally arriving half an hour later at the border proper. It was seven-thirty and night had fallen. Bissau itself was another three hours by bus, which I would tackle in the morning just as my motorcycle driver would be embarking on his return journey, but lighter without me on the back. It was much labour for little reward but then perhaps he was 'lucky' to have secured the 'contract' ahead of his rivals, such is the wretched condition of the majority of those born into the richest continent. But let me not overlabour the point; we, too, must take our share of the blame, and perhaps we are beginning to do so at long last.

*

At just CFA3,750/£4.50 by coach, the price from Banjul to Bamako was ridiculously cheap given the 800 miles we were about to traverse, compounded by the exceptionally bad state of the roads in most of Mali itself, which was by far most of the journey. We left at dusk and reached the border with Senegal shortly after midnight, only to have to wait until dawn before the border post opened; even then, the formalities were tedious, as they were again on the other side. From there to the border with Mali was only three hours but, again, we were delayed for over two hours while officials boarded the coach in search of single young men, who had previously been asked to come down by the driver but to leave their luggage behind, including my immediate neighbour. It later transpired that they might have been denied entry into Mali for a reason I couldn't fathom, until we picked them up a mile or so after we had cleared immigration.

And so began the tedious night-long journey, made more so by the frequent stops for prayers, which hadn't happened on my previous journeys but now we were in wholly Muslim territory. Just before dusk, we were joined by two armed soldiers; it seemed that we were also entering potential terrorist terrain. All night, we crawled through the sparse landscape of the Sahel, defined by Wikipedia as 'the transition zone between the more humid Sudanian savannas to its south and the drier Sahara to the north,' and where it took just four days for my lips to crack from the lack of moisture in the air. Fortunately, there was a full moon, which gave greater majesty to the frequent clusters of the magnificent baobab trees that so casually dominated a landscape of otherwise sparse vegetation. The world's largest and longest-living flowering plant—Zimbabwe in southern Africa claims the oldest at 2,450 years—they can grow up to 100 feet high and half as wide. They also look as if they were planted the wrong way around, hence the legends surrounding them. The people along the Zambezi River, for example, believe that in the early days they were proud and upright, lording it over smaller plants, but that the gods became angry with their attitude and uprooted them before planting them back with their roots facing upwards. Another legend has it that they were too adventurous and kept wandering between continents—they also grow in Australia—until one day God decided enough was enough and flipped them upside down. To the San peoples of the Kalahari, 'the God Thora took a dislike to the specimen in their wonderful garden and threw it over that wall of Paradise to Earth, where it landed upside down but nonetheless continued to grow'.[3] Whatever the case, the tree is central to the region's ecosystem. They are 'fundamental to the entire dry African savannah' because they 'help keep soil conditions humid, aid nutrient recycling, and slow erosion with their massive root system'. They are also 'an essential source of water and shelter for hundreds of animals, including birds, lizards, monkeys, and even elephants'. For humans specifically, the 'fruit pulp can be eaten, soaked in water to make a refreshing drink, preserved into a jam, or roasted and ground to make a coffee-like substance'; their bark can also can 'be pounded to make everything from rope, mats, and baskets to paper and cloth', and their leaves 'can be boiled and eaten, or glue can be made from their flower's pollen'.[4]

Their massive trunks can hold up to 32,000 gallons of water, which means they can survive almost any drought; additionally, their barks are fireproof. Alas, it seems that climate change is wreaking its own havoc, here as in the Los Angeles that is 'burn, baby, burn' at the time of writing as we enter The Second Coming of President Trump in which mere anarchy is about to loosed upon the world: nine of the continent's thirteen oldest and largest baobabs have died in the past decade as a result of warming temperatures, which 'made them weaker and more susceptible to drought, diseases, fire, or wind,' but then why believe the 'woke' science? Within hours of being sworn in, the leader of the biggest polluter on earth promptly signed an executive order directing the US to once again withdraw from the 'landmark' Paris climate agreement, in the process 'dealing a blow to worldwide efforts to combat global warming and once again distancing the US from its closest allies'.[5] Following this news, a leading global scientist stated that to keep warming under 2 degrees Celsius by 2100, as envisaged in the 2015 Paris climate accord, is now an impossible scenario.[6]

Naturally, a tree so central to the well-being of those living in its vicinity is attributed magical properties. For some, a baby boy washed in water that has soaked its bark will grow up strong and mighty, like the tree itself. Again, people living around the Limpopo River believe that women who live in villages where the trees are plentiful will have more children, and science would seem to agree given that soups made from its leaves are rich in vitamins and might therefore render them more fertile. But these are folk tales. What is surprising is that it doesn't seem to have featured in modern African literature (where descriptions of the natural world generally don't anyway).

10

A NATION IS NOT BUILT ON INDISCIPLINE AND DISORDER

And now, at the risk of hyperbole, all three of the Sahel states appear to have found their human baobabs that the wider continent has signalled it desperately craves. In the eyes of their people they stand taller and prouder than their contemporaries by demonstrating that the apparent decades of drought in which only a few drank champagne while 'the people' were denied clean drinking water (to quote the late Thomas Sankara, of whom more presently) were actually a long delayed rallying cry. Just as we thought we had finally put paid to the military lording it over us as we embrace the brave new world of one person, one vote, they also all happen to be soldiers.

Mali's Colonel Assimi Goïta originally served as leader of the National Committee for the Salvation of the People, a group of rebels who staged a coup d'état in 2020 against the democratically elected government of Ibrahim Boubacar Keïta. To satisfy ECOWAS demands concerning the sanctity of the democratic imperative, Goïta was named vice-president under a civilian president, Bah Ndaw, with the promise to hold fresh elections within eighteen months. Goïta himself retained the power to decide ministerial appointments, which effectively allowed military control of the government, and which inevitably led to tensions within the cabinet. However, even before the time was up the military staged another coup, claiming that Ndaw was trying to 'sabotage' the transition programme by attempting a cabinet reshuffle that would have excluded the soldiers. Ndaw was arrested but later released. In June 2023, a referendum apparently supported by ninety-seven per cent of the electorate adopted a new constitution, whereupon the constitutional court ruled that Goïta should carry the title 'president of the transition, head of state' in order that he might 'lead the transition process to its conclusion'.[1] The following year, Goïta promoted himself to General of the Malian Army and remained silent on any impending democracy, but then it turns out that the Malian people might not themselves yearn for such; according to a 'fastidious nationwide survey' carried out in 2021 by researchers at the Bamako office of the Netherlands Institute for Multiparty Democracy:

> The survey divides Mali into 'cultural regions' defined by history and geography—a better model than ethnicity. In every region, researchers found a widespread aversion to one person, one vote representative democracy. My first thought was that this was a reactionary view, based on the belief that some voices should count for more than others. In fact, one person, one vote makes no sense to people in Mali because it insists that majority opinion is the only way to adjudicate daunting issues of justice and power in a complex, heterogeneous society. The principle of justice in old Sahelian regimes, though it might be honoured in the breach, is that each person must get something and no one should walk away empty-handed. The most persistent criticism of electoral democracy in the region—not just in Mali, but in Niger and Burkina—is that it breeds exclusion, barring the defeated from any share in the spoils or decisions, while the winners rejoice in victory

for 'notre régime, notre pouvoir'. In the West, the despotism of the majority and the ritual of gracefully conceding defeat are (or used to be) part of the political culture. For many Sahelians, they look like a recipe for conflict and division.[2]

'In Bamako' appeared in the *London Review of Books* in 2023 as a 'Diary' by Rahmane Idrissa, the Nigérien 'political scientist fast embracing history,' according to his entry on the website of Leiden University, where he teaches, and is supported in a subsequent letter from a long-term 'Western' observer of the region:

> Idrissa puts his finger on one of the things I regret, looking back at my own fifteen years with a conflict-prevention NGO and, before that, 25 years as a foreign correspondent for American and British publications: the complacency with which we put elections before all else when gauging progress in less privileged, crisis-prone countries. We wanted those elections free, we wanted them fair, we wanted them transparent. We demanded electoral reform, independent electoral commissions and level electoral playing fields. What we never wanted to do was question the usefulness and suitability of having those elections in the first place. It never occurred to us to ask whether elections might actually be causing the violence we were talking about, rather than ending it. We assumed that elections meant democracy and peaceful outcomes.

He also points out that, in the 'richer countries of the global north', elections 'work admirably to produce elite-run oligarchies or, in the US case, something more like a plutarchy,' which would seem to be admirably proven by the new presidency of Donald Trump currently preparing to acquire Gaza as a 'big real estate site', along with Greenland and Canada for their vast mineral resources (to say nothing of the world's 'security').

As things stand, Goïta is not in a hurry to go anywhere and 'the people' don't seem in a hurry to have him leave. The same is equally true of Niger's General Abdourahamane Tchiani, former head of the presidential guard who overthrew President Mohamed Bazoum in 2023, ostensibly because he was about to be replaced following strained relations between them. Proclaiming himself president of the National Council for the Safeguard of the Homeland, he claimed the coup was undertaken to avoid 'the gradual and inevitable demise' of the country, Bazoum having tried to hide 'the harsh reality', which he called 'a pile of dead, displaced, humiliation and frustration'.[3] He also proposed a three-year window for a transition to civilian rule. Bazoum himself remains in detention and is allowed only occasional calls to family and friends. Again, 'the people' seem sanguine about the military in power, even coming out in unprecedented numbers when President Macron initially attempted to defy Tchiani's order to close France's military bases in the country; but more popular by far than either Goïta or Tchiani is Captain Ibrahim Traoré of Burkina Faso, the youngest of the three (and the second youngest in the world after Iceland's current prime minister, Kristrún Frostadóttir) who is worshipped by Africa's youths heartily sick of the old men intent on dragging them to the grave, à la Mo Ibrahim.

Traoré was part of the group of army officers who supported the January 2022 coup d'état by the Patriotic Movement for Safeguard and Restoration. A second coup followed nine months later when it became obvious that their initial leader, Paul-Henri Sandaogo Damiba, was unable to contain the jihadist insurgency that was their main focus. According to Traoré, he and the mainly junior officers who had fought against the jihadist insurgency at the frontlines tried to get Damiba to 'refocus' on the rebellion but eventually overthrew him because 'his ambitions were diverting away from what we set out to do'.[4] Traoré was then chosen as the new head and initially promised to hold democratic elections in July 2024 but then changed his mind on the grounds that they would be meaningless until the insurgency was contained following national consultations boycotted by most political parties. Traoré's mandate was then extended for an additional five years while also allowing him to contest the next presidential election when the time comes.

From the beginning, Traoré made it clear that he was following the path laid out by his slain predecessor, the equally youthful—and equally charismatic—Thomas Sankara, the one who changed the country's colonial name from Upper Volta to Burkina Faso (variously 'land of the upright people' and 'home of the people of integrity') for which he also wrote the anthem, the first verse of which perfectly captures the spirit of what he was about:

> Against the humiliating rule of a thousand years ago,
> the rapacity that came from afar to enslave them a hundred years
> ago.
> Against cynical malice metamorphosed
> into neocolonialism and its small local servants, many faltered and
> some resisted.
> But failures, successes, sweat, blood
> have strengthened our courageous people and fertilised their
> heroic struggle...

Many believe he was assassinated in 1987 after just four years in power with the alleged collusion of his deputy and 'brother' from before-before, Blaise Compaoré, on the orders of the then French president, François Mitterrand. It happened that the latter, perhaps intrigued by the new kid on the block, paid Sankara a visit a year before, only to be publicly lectured by him on the 'insouciance of the French, who have no qualms about receiving visits from white supremacists and their allies':

> And so it is in this context, Monsieur François Mitterrand, that we have not understood how bandits such as Jonas Savimbi, killers like

Pieter Botha, have had the right to rove across France... They have stained it with their hands and with their feet, which are covered in blood. And all those who have allowed them to act as they have will carry the full responsibility, here and elsewhere, today and for ever.[5]

Mitterrand was initially taken aback and then abandoned his prepared speech to patronise the young man:

President Sankara is a bit of a disturbing man! It's true, he titillates you, he asks questions... With him, it is not easy to sleep in peace: he does not leave you with a clear conscience! I, on this point, am like him. He needs to know that I'm just like him, thirty-five years older. He says what he thinks, I say it too. And I find that in some judgments, he has the sharpness of a beautiful youth and the merit of a Head of State totally devoted to his people. I admire his qualities, which are great, but he cuts too thin; in my opinion, it goes further than it needs to. May he allow me to speak to him in the name of my experience.[6]

In footage of the event, he's then seen to place an avuncular hand on his shoulder and Sankara laughs but doesn't look up. Less than a year later, Sankara was shot dead in his office along with twelve of his aides. Attempts to investigate the details have never got anywhere, but before dawn the following morning the corpses had been buried in a common grave. According to James Brooke, an American journalist based in the subregion for Radio France International, the burial was so hasty that mourners were able to dip their handkerchiefs in pools of blood draining from the grave.

Compaoré himself went on to rule for twenty-seven years before he was in turn overthrown after attempting to alter the constitution to extend his term. (He subsequently fled to Côte d'Ivoire, where he was given asylum by Alassane Ouattara, presumably on the orders of the then French president, François Hollande.) Many fear the same fate will befall Traoré, who has apparently survived at least nineteen such attempts as of May

A NATION IS NOT BUILT ON INDISCIPLINE AND DISORDER

2025. Indeed, he is like a modern version of the legendary Captain Tomba, an eighteenth-century chief in what was to become Sierra Leone 'of a tall strong make and bold stern aspect' who railed against the slave trade and forbade his subjects to partake in it, even punishing those who worked with the European merchants. Because of his stand, he was eventually captured by European traders (with likely help from rival villages) and singled out by his new 'master':

> This fellow seemed to disdain the other slaves for their readiness to be examined and scorned to look at the Buyers, refusing to rise or stretch out his limbs as his master commanded. This got him an unmerciful whipping, with a cutting manatea strap, from his master's own hand... The Negro bore it all with magnanimity, shrinking very little, but shed a tear or two which he endeavoured to hide as though ashamed of.

A few days into the voyage, he and two companions—one of them was a woman—led a revolt which killed three of the sailors. They were eventually overpowered but his life was spared for fear that killing him might lead to a greater revolt. He survived the trip across the Atlantic Ocean and was sold in Kingston, Jamaica, along with 189 people, and that was the last anyone heard of him. Given that transporting Africans to the New World is now verboten, it will be something of a miracle if Traoré himself is still alive by the time you are reading this.

The most obvious sign of continuity was Traoré's appointment of Apollinaire J. Kyélam de Tambèla, a staunch supporter of Sankara, as prime minister to oversee the 'refoundation of the nation'. One of his first actions was to call for a reduction in the salaries of the president and ministers; in his words: 'I have already said that Burkina Faso cannot be developed outside the path set by Thomas Sankara.' Variously described as a lawyer, pan-Africanist, writer and statesman, he had previously been instrumental in forging a strong relationship with Nicaragua, as evinced in Sankara's speech at the United Nations General Assembly in 1984, where he declared, in part: 'I wish also to feel close to my comrades of Nicaragua, whose ports are being mined, whose towns are being bombed and who, despite all, face up with courage and lucidity to their fate. I suffer with all those in Latin America who are suffering from imperialist domination.'[7] Two years later, Sankara travelled to the country to personally visit Daniel Ortega, the Sandinista leader (he also took the opportunity to visit Cuba's Fidel Castro, another of his heroes); Ortega returned the favour that same year. And now the bond was renewed, as Tambèla made clear in a speech in the Nicaraguan capital, Managua in 2023 (where he also had high praise for Iran):

> For people of my generation, there are things that unite us with Nicaragua, Augusto César Sandino, the Sandinista National Liberation Front and Commander Daniel Ortega.
>
> We have learned to know Nicaragua. When the liberation struggle began, I was small, but we followed, day by day, the context of Nicaragua's liberation. I went in July of '79, and when they entered Managua we were happy, people of my age celebrated that...
>
> And then, when Thomas Sankara came to power, Daniel Ortega and the Sandinista Revolution was something happy for us; we as students studied a lot the history of Nicaragua, we followed its evolution.[8]

He added that Burkina Faso supported Nicaragua in its International Court of Justice case against the United States, where Washington was found guilty of illegally sponsoring far right 'contra' death squads, which waged a war of terror against the government that included mining the country's ports. Nicaragua duly won the case in 1986, but the US is yet to pay a single cent on a judgment by a court that the same US under President Trump not only doesn't recognise but further insulted when he signed an executive order cutting US financial assistance to South Africa following its genocide case against Netanyahu and Gallant. Coincidentally, Trump also prioritised the US resettlement of white Afrikaner South African 'refugees' apparently suffering from what he called 'government-sponsored race-based discrimination,' but as commentators were quick to point out, white South Africans make up just eight per cent of the country's population but own seventy-two per cent of its farmland as part of the continuing legacy of an apartheid that formally ended three decades ago. For its part, South African government officials have denied private land confiscations or racially motivated discrimination, but are merely looking at unused or publicly owned land to give to deserving citizens.

Many reactionaries unable to deal with the contradictions of the otherwise glorious history of European slavery and colonialism they once celebrated as bringing light to the dark places of the earth, and who now describe as 'woke' those who would question this history with the kind of intellectual rigour they should otherwise celebrate for what it is, will no doubt deplore anyone with an enduring soft spot for Castro who, along with Libya's Muammar Gaddafi and Yasser Arafat of the Palestinian Liberation Organization, supported the cause in South Africa 'to the hilt' (in the words of Nelson Mandela) by supplying the arms it needed. Castro went further again than the other two by putting boots on the ground (even against the wishes of the then Soviet Union), an act that was decisive in turning the tide. Nigeria, meanwhile, the giant of Africa, fought the apartheid regime with 'ordinary mouth' while its otherwise idle soldiers in the barracks flogged 'bloody civilians' in the street for jumping the queue at the bus stop, or for failing to use overhead foot bridges. But what is one to say—what would the Ukrainians say—about Traoré's embrace of Putin at the 2023 Second Russia–Africa Summit in St Petersburg: 'There is a desire to change politics which leads us to turn our backs to our traditional partners and turn towards our true friends like Russia, who supported us from the times of decolonisation until today.' He also assured Putin of the 'support of Burkina Faso, its people and its government' given what Russia 'is currently experiencing with its special military operation.'[9] Mali's Colonel Assimi Goïta mimicked the sentiments: 'I had a rich telephone conversation with H.E. Vladimir Putin. We discussed ways and means to strengthen bilateral cooperation, particularly economic and security. I welcome a win-win partnership based on mutual respect.'[10]

It is true that the fact that the suffocatingly self-righteous White Western Christian Civilisation (which is to say those who agree with the apartheid state of Israel that Hamas is a 'terrorist' organisation, precisely what they once labelled South Africa's now ruling African National Congress)—i.e. Australia, Canada, the EU, New Zealand, the UK and the US (along with honorary white Japan)—preaches human rights and a rules-based world order based on respect for international law even as it enables genocide doesn't thereby make its 'enemies' any less palatable. Tambèla's high praise for Ortega was perhaps commendable in 1984 but what are we to say about his regime four decades later? In his first, youthful incarnation from 1985 to 1990, he continued the work he had started over the previous six years as Coordinator of the Junta of National Reconstruction, namely land reform, wealth redistribution and literacy programmes, even as the government faced a rebellion by US-backed rebels. It was held that illiteracy rates fell from fifty to thirteen per cent, and although many considered these figures excessive, the country was awarded the 1980 UNESCO Nadezhda K. Krupskaya Literacy Prize in recognition of its achievement. Two years later, the World Health Organization deemed Nicaragua a model for primary health care, particularly through vaccination campaigns and the construction of public hospitals, which halved child mortality.

A NATION IS NOT BUILT ON INDISCIPLINE AND DISORDER

Despite all this, Ortega lost the 1996 and 2001 elections but won again in 2006 and remains in office as I write following a constitutional amendment in 2014 allowing him to run for an unlimited number of five-year terms on the grounds of promoting 'stability'; he subsequently took 'full control of all four branches of government, state institutions, the military and police.'[11] Trouble erupted in 2018 following student demonstrations, whereupon 'the former revolutionary leader' revealed himself 'more like a cartel boss than a president,' according to Tim Rogers in *The Atlantic*:

> Over the past seven weeks, Ortega's police and paramilitaries have killed more than 120 people, mostly students and other young protesters who are demanding the president's ouster and a return to democracy, according to a human-rights group. Police hunt students like enemy combatants. Sandinista Youth paramilitaries, armed and paid by Ortega's party, drive around in pickup trucks attacking protesters. Gangs of masked men loot and burn shops with impunity. Cops wear civilian clothing, and some paramilitaries dress in police uniforms. 'This is starting to look more like Syria than Caracas,' one Nicaraguan business leader told me.[12]

None of this is new in the world, although his Burkinabe friend, who was subsequently relieved of his post when Traoré dissolved the government in December 2024, might be interested to know that among the usual suspects singled out for persecution—students, activists, opposition politicians—are indigenous people and *people of African descent*, as we continue to delude ourselves that others have our best interests at heart, which they don't, meaning that we are on our own and the sooner we grasp that the sooner we will end our centuries-long slavery. For his part, Ortega told then President Mahmoud Ahmadinejad on an official visit to Iran in 2006 that the 'revolutions' in their respective countries 'are about justice, liberty, self-determination, and the struggle against imperialism,'[13] although I suspect many Iranians living under this 'revolution' of so many fine abstractions would disagree. These might include, for instance, the family and friends of Mahsa Amini, the twenty-two-year-old who was beaten to death by the 'morality police' for not wearing her hijab just so, or those of the Kurdish women's rights activist Varisheh Moradi, and Pakhshan Azizi, a Kurdish-Iranian social worker, both of whom are currently facing the death penalty for 'armed activities against the Islamic republic,' but perhaps I am simply being naive; perhaps I am missing the bigger picture.

Traoré, for his part, has nonetheless undertaken a number of measures for which he is rightly lauded. It isn't only that he has called out France's policies towards its colonies but that he has directly impacted the lives of ordinary Burkinabes in ways which only seem remarkable in the African context but would be taken as merely responsible governance elsewhere. Among the most far-reaching are free education up to and including university level on the grounds that 'an educated nation cannot be enslaved'; eighty-five 'autonomous water points' that provide clean drinking water nationwide, thereby combating waterborne diseases; streamlining the previously sluggish and bloated bureaucracy to ensure that projects are completed on time and at cost; and paying proper attention to agriculture, the backbone of the country's economy that has been undermined by so-called aid, the debilitating effects of which were perfectly summed up by Sankara:

> They have not helped us develop. They have instead created a beggar mentality. We hold out our hands to receive food. That is not a good thing. Those who really want to help us can give us ploughs, tractors, fertilizer, insecticide, watering cans, drills, dams. That is how we would define food aid. Those who come with wheat, millet, corn or milk, they are not helping us.[14]

To date, the government 'has distributed over 400 tractors, 239 tillers, 710 motor pumps, and 714 motorcycles to support rural farmers.' By providing access to improved seeds and farm inputs, Traoré has 'spearheaded a surge in agricultural output. Tomato production rose from 315,000 metric tonnes in 2022 to 360,000 in 2024, millet increased from 907,000 to 1.1 million metric tonnes, and rice production grew from 280,000 to 326,000 metric tonnes'.[15] He has also modernised the road network to make it easier to move goods and people, as I saw for myself when I crossed over from Mali. Where, in Mali, everywhere was littered with the ubiquitous pure water sachets that distressed me so on the slave beach in Lagos at the start of this journey, I hardly saw any in all the 550 miles from the border to Ouagadougou, the capital, and then the 470 miles from there to the border with Togo on my way back home. Again, unlike Mali, the villages we passed through were spotless, evidence that ordinary Burkinabes took a greater pride in their surroundings.

More significantly perhaps, the government is in the process of building a gold refining factory to maximise the international price of the country's most valuable raw material; according to the Société nationale des substances précieuses:

> This major project will be carried out as part of a strategic partnership with MARENA GOLD company, which already has a refinery in Mali. The refinery will have a refining capacity of 400 kilograms/day and will be built on an area of five (05) hectares. This refinery, which could become the home of gold, is a complex that also includes a jewellery store, storage warehouses, security premises and administrative buildings, including the future headquarters of the National precious substances company.[16]

Previously, gold was exported unrefined at $4 per ounce; refined, it would be worth double that. Traoré is also seeking to repatriate the country's gold reserves held abroad, mostly in the US, as are those of a number of other African countries.

Looking back, the only wonder is that it has taken this long for a former colony to do what should have been done at independence six decades earlier and, in doing it, to break a jinx we hardly knew we lived under. Equally boldly, and just as timely, he has also rejected the external loans that keep the continent in hock to foreign creditors; as he bluntly put it: 'Africa doesn't need the World Bank, IMF, Europe, or America.'[17] There were also reports that the country had cleared its US$4.7 billion external debt, which would be in keeping with a leader who clearly puts his country ahead of his ego; and although there is some doubt that he was able to do this given the parlous state of the country's finances, there is no doubt that the new Nigerian government of President Bọ́lá Ahmed Tinúbú borrowed US$6.45 billion in its first sixteen months to pay for, amongst other things, 469 Toyota Land Cruisers for all federal lawmakers at a total cost of US$25 million.

Finally, all three Sahel countries not only announced their intention to leave ECOWAS but, additionally, do away with the CFA franc and establish their own currency. To this end, they signed the Liptako-Gourma Charter establishing the tripartite Alliance of Sahel States, with the agreement that 'any attack on the sovereignty and territorial integrity of one or more contracted parties will be considered an act of aggression against the other parties.'[18] In fact, they had already signalled their intention to leave ECOWAS just before I left for my trip and which came into force one year later, after which I had safely returned, which in effect made me a witness to history but without the need for a visa.

The problem started when ECOWAS suspended Niger and imposed sanctions against it in August 2023 following Tchiani's coup, as it had previously done with Mali in 2021 and Burkina

Faso the year after for their own military coups. According to Nigerian President Tinúbú, who also happened to be the new ECOWAS chair, the point about the sanctions was to reaffirm 'our relentless commitment to democracy, human rights, and the well-being of the people of Niger,'[19] in keeping with the 2001 good governance protocol, although for Traoré and his fellow Sahelian rulers, he is hardly qualified to lecture anybody on what Fẹlá Kútì, the late Afrobeat musician, called 'Democrazy/Crazy Demo' for reasons alluded to earlier. Moreover, the Niger sanctions seemed particularly vicious given that Article 68 of the 1993 revised ECOWAS treaty takes into consideration 'the economic and social difficulties that may arise in certain Member States, particularly island and land-locked States.' The most egregious result was to cut off the eighty-five per cent of the power that Nigeria supplies its northern neighbour in return for its historical decision not to dam the Niger River even though the country nevertheless pays for it at commercial rates. The other was to close the 1,200-mile-long border and thereby deprive the country access to the port of Lagos along with the market which constitutes sixty per cent of its GDP. According to USAID, Nigeria is 'critical for Niger to stabilize prices and supplies,' being 'the primary source of demand for livestock'.[20] As Traoré fumed: 'Thousands of Nigériens died on their hospital beds because of a lack of electricity or lack of medicine. It is a crime! They are responsible for these sanctions; they are responsible for these deaths.'[21]

ECOWAS itself, which quickly realised it had blundered, pointed out that the revised treaty required the Sahelian states to give one year's notice before they ceased to be members. For Traoré, this was just so much pedantry: 'It's not out of the blue to turn your back on an organization, but the result of a thorough analysis. If it were a fit of anger, we would have done it a long time ago. We took time to analyse the situation, weigh a lot of things and finally make a decision.'[22] His main grouse was ECOWAS's failure to help curb the Islamic insurgencies plaguing all three countries despite the provisions of the community's charter: 'For more than a decade, Mali and Niger have been at war with terrorism. And in Burkina Faso, we've been at war for almost a decade. We have never received any aid from this organization.'[23]

The same went for France, whose military had supposedly been operating in the subregion since January 2013 following an upsurge in violence as a result of a $15 million donation two years earlier from the Emir of Qatar to burgeoning Islamist movements across northern Mali and the Sahel generally. Operation Sérval was initially successful in containing the extremist threat in Mali's north and subsequently transitioned into Operation Barkhane the following year to encompass Burkina Faso, Niger, Chad and Mauritania. However, it lacked a clear counterterrorism direction and appeared bogged down: as of October 2023, non-state armed groups controlled eighty per cent of Mali's central and northern regions, and forty per cent of Burkina Faso. This fed into the growing resentment against existing French neo-imperialism already alluded to, which is why its leaders turned to Russia and, to a lesser extent, China. Macron tried at first to resist the move by claiming that France was only in the Sahel 'because there is a terrorist threat, and sovereign states asked us to help,' but when his hand was finally forced he proceeded to sneer at the 'baroque alliance between self-proclaimed pan-Africans' and Russian and Chinese 'neo-imperialists,' both of whom were stirring up old arguments over sovereignty and colonial exploitation for their own ends—as who should know.[24] Even worse for Macron, the triumvirate believed—with good reason—that President Tinúbú had sought to invade Niger at the behest of France, which is even more worried about the loss of its colonies.

There are also rumours that French troops are currently embedded in northern Nigeria, ostensibly to overthrow the Niger junta, but this is impossible to verify, although it wouldn't be the first time foreign troops were invited onto Nigerian soil. The former president, Goodluck Jonathan, once engaged Executive Outcomes, a firm of mercenaries run by a former South African Defence Force officer, Eeben Barlow, to help the army curb the activities of the Boko Haram terrorists. Between them, they racked up some notable successes, exposing problems within the Nigerian army as they did so. 'We've been on the terrain for two months,' Idriss Déby, the president of Chad, complained, 'and we haven't seen a single Nigerian soldier. There is a definite deficit of co-ordination and a lack of common action.'[25] Barlow himself let slip that he thought the Nigerian army was incompetent: 'Foreign armies...have spent considerable time in Nigeria where "window-dressing training" has been the order of the day. But look through the window and the room is empty.' A 'senior Western diplomat' (no one ever quotes senior non-Western diplomats, but there we go) told the *New York Times* that the mercenaries were playing 'a major operational role' carrying out night attacks on Boko Haram and that 'the next morning the Nigerian army rolls in and claims success'.[26]

Russian intervention, of course, means the Wagner Group, the Russian state-funded private military company which has been operating in the continent since 2018 and has to date made a fortune mining the continent's abundant minerals. In the Central African Republic alone, it controls a gold mine capable of producing 'upwards of $1bn' annually; according to an eyewitness who was forced to flee the town of Bambari in early 2021: 'They were shooting us from the ground, and planes fired from the sky... To say "killing" is an understatement. It was total carnage. Like Armageddon.'[27] The group's first, flamboyant commander, Yevgeny Prigozhin, who was killed in a plane crash in 2023 following an astonishingly ill-judged rebellion against President Putin, his benefactor, claimed they were a more wholesome alternative to 'the former colonizers...filling these countries with terrorists...creating a colossal security crisis,'[28] which perhaps sounded attractive to the Sahelian triumvirate. If so, they are making a costly mistake, in Mali's case to the tune of $10 million monthly to maintain Wagner's 1,000 troops in a country where any number of unemployed young men can more than cover the price—and then some—if given the proper training. As one US researcher put it, Wagner's relationship with the Sahel is 'simple supply and demand: African putschists need the security that Wagner can provide, and the Kremlin needs the funding stream to soften the blow from biting Western sanctions,' which makes it no different from its 'Western' counterparts.[29] And why should it be any different? Why should foreigners have Africa's best interests at heart when Africans themselves show contempt for each other—and therefore themselves?

And then there are Traoré's own incipient dictatorial tendencies, inevitable in one with absolute power and the enduring problem with the experience of military rule we seem intent on forgetting in our quest for the messiah who will magically solve our myriad problems. So how different is Traoré from the usual run of our political leaders? It seems that he shares the widespread distaste for 'homosexuality and related practices,' which are prohibited and punishable by law, according to a 2025 decree for a new Personal and Family Code. This is entirely in keeping with most governments in sub-Saharan Africa (whatever their ostensible political colouring), the continuing legacy of what the Irish writer Anne Enright called 'the feminizing insult that is colonialism'; that, indeed, they are men, as I saw firsthand with my own father because the White Man had apparently signed a piece of paper granting him 'independence', as if the White Man hadn't signed all sorts of pieces of paper that nonetheless kept him subjugated.

The desired macho image also caused Traoré to threaten to conscript magistrates and judges who ruled against the government into the so-called Volunteers for the Defence of the Homeland for two years, as he has already done with journalists for publishing 'negative' articles; according to Reporters sans Frontières:

> 'There is a journalist who was recently conscripted because, since 2023, he has spent his time lying,' Captain Ibrahim Traoré declared shortly after a speech to the Burkinabe public... The junta leader's statement acted as both a warning to media professionals and a confirmation that a journalist—potentially Atiana Serge Oulon, editor of the fortnightly *L'Événement* who was kidnapped by alleged members of the National Intelligence Agency on 24 June—had been conscripted into the army.
>
> The head of state also stated that the journalist in question 'has been summoned by the gendarmerie [a division of the armed forces], by the ASCE-LC [Superior State Control and Anti-Corruption Authority] and by all structures to provide proof of what he is saying.' The questioning process described is remarkably similar to the multiple summons sent to Serge Oulon after his report on suspected embezzlement within the militia, published in December 2022. When contacted for further details, a source close to the President's office said that RSF should 'stick to what the President says.' A few days earlier, however, this same source had told RSF that 'Serge was safe.'[30]

According to Traoré, 'individual freedoms [are] not superior to national freedom' because 'a nation is not built on indiscipline and disorder.'[31] He also declared that no country in history developed under a democratic system, and that Burkina Faso was in the middle of a 'popular, progressive revolution'. To that end, not even medical doctors are safe from conscription in a country which is at the very bottom of the global rankings for doctor–patient ratio, ahead only of the Democratic Republic of the Congo and behind even Afghanistan. Dr Arouna Louré, the physician in question, was attending to patients in the operating theatre at a hospital in Ouagadougou when armed soldiers burst through the door without warning. 'They made me understand they could make me leave using the gentle or the violent method,'[32] he told the BBC, whereupon he was bundled into a van and transported to a military training camp hundreds of miles away.

Dr Louré said he received minimal combat training but, fortunately, was not involved in any fighting during the ninety-four days he was on the frontline, instead treating soldiers, mostly for malaria. Later, a civil society group challenged the conscription of some of its members in court after they received call-up papers shortly after announcing plans to hold a demonstration against the restriction of freedoms, with the court ruling their conscription illegal; according to one of their lawyers, Guy Hervé Kam: 'We were able to demonstrate that this deployment was unnecessary and served as a punishment.' However, the junta appealed against the ruling and arrested Mr Kam himself, who remains in custody as I write. Dr Louré, meanwhile, who is back home with his family, said that the goal 'is to humiliate. If you obey, they take a photo of you and post it on social media... If you flee the country, they'll call you a coward. And if you sue the state, people will say that you are a coward too.' He remains active on social media and is optimistic about the country's future even as he deplored 'the overall strategy of the government, corruption, illicit enrichment and nepotism. That doesn't happen at the front, but rather in Ouagadougou.'

No, I don't like military rule under whatever guise and no matter how supposedly 'charismatic' the leader, but let me leave the last word on this topic to the historian Samuel Fury Childs Daly in his 2024 book *Soldier's Paradise: Militarism in Africa after Empire*:

> Soldiers run countries like they fight wars. Combat is their metaphor for politics. They approach political problems like battles to be won or lost, even when it isn't clear what winning or losing would mean.

A NATION IS NOT BUILT ON INDISCIPLINE AND DISORDER

They treat their rivals like enemies—not people who see things differently but adversaries who have to be defeated. They divvy up the population into friends and foes and treat them accordingly. They enforce conformity, and they try to make everyone think like they do. They put up a united front, but behind the scenes they plot against one another—each wants to be the alpha.[33]

It is a symptom of sub-Saharan Africa's desperate condition that Traoré is feted as the saviour we desperately crave, having so quickly forgotten why we temporarily succeeded in ridding ourselves of the soldiers who turned us into second-class citizens in our own countries. But then, alas, it seems that we need it; we need to be kicked up the backside by a small pikin (to use the local patois) in military uniform before we finally wake up to the pitiful condition that we find ourselves in, which is akin to slavery, but which we have colluded in realising, if only we will take responsibility.

EPILOGUE

'Fucking Africans.' Thus Joni, my Ghanaian friend from my previous life in the UK, whom I stayed with in Accra just a week into my journey for this book. Like me, he had relocated back home, in his case to a three-bedroom bungalow he had bought not long after I had myself returned to battle for the apartment left me by my father. Like me, he was in the enviable position of enjoying a British pension as well as access to the National Health Service for the price of a return ticket and so was far better off than his contemporaries who had remained behind. However low sterling sunk, you could be sure that the local currency would always be weaker, sometimes catastrophically so, as in fact happened to the Nigerian currency, which was devalued by a factor of three following the removal of the long-standing fuel subsidy on the instructions of the World Bank (or was it the IMF: same difference) shortly after I returned to the country at the end of my journey. So why the subsidy in the first place?

The answer goes to the heart of our malaise. Nigeria is the world's seventh-largest producer of crude oil. There are four refineries supposedly operated by a government quango which together employ 1,604 staff at a cost of ₦137bn/£63m per annum, yet between them produce not a single drop of refined, and this despite regular turn-around maintenance grants of up to £1.5m a time. Meanwhile, the people 'chopping' from these grants also happen to own refineries abroad dedicated to supplying the Nigerian market, mainly in Belgium and the Netherlands, with sulphur levels of 2,044 parts per million (the limit for diesel and gasoline sold in the EU is 10 ppm). As one commentator put it, 'Nigeria exports high-quality low-sulphur crude and imports low-quality high-sulphur fuel.'[1] The result is a country ruled by a cabal—the five richest men are worth $30bn between them, courtesy of the $20 trillion stolen from the treasury between 1960 and 2005—that delivers some of the worst air pollution in the world. The Dutch regulatory agency, the Inspectie Leefomgeving en Transport, was subsequently 'in dialogue with the producers' to ensure that the Netherlands only exports fuel 'in line with the European quality requirements'. The Belgium authorities were even tardier to react but then this is Africa so what does it matter, especially since the indigenes themselves don't give a toss.

'Fucking Africans,' Joni repeated under his breath as we sat in short sleeves and slippers in the garden of his local bar watching the early evening news in the company of Kabral Blay-Amihere, the journalist I had met in London when he fled the Rawlings government for a spell at the London School of Economics, and whom I later teamed up with back in Ghana when I visited the country to write about the plight of the press that had reduced him to publishing a weekly sports paper. Fortunately, he had done well in the intervening years following a regime change (such is the volatility of the subregion's politics), becoming the country's high commissioner to Sierra Leone in 2001 for four years, the very year his former tormentor finally stepped down, followed by a stint as ambassador to Côte d'Ivoire for another four. He had also published three books. Meeting up again after all these years, I was tempted to wax lyrical about the transient nature of time, as in, 'You do not even know what will happen tomorrow! What is your life? You are a mist that appears for a little while and then vanishes,' but Joni just shrugged impatiently. He was even more despondent than I was at the announcement by Nigeria's Appeal Court declaring Tinúbú's victory in the sham presidential election I hadn't wanted to witness back home.

'Fucking Africans,' he said for the third time as he called for another round of beer and proceeded to name the myriad traits that were holding us back: ethnicity, lack of political consciousness and nationalism; uncontrolled corruption, nepotism and materialism; religiosity. I well understood his frustration given my own gloom about this latest development but made worse, in his case, by his earlier left-leaning idealism that had originally carried him to Europe in his mid-twenties. For myself, I was never a joiner although some of the people I hung out with during my undergraduate days in Swansea in the mid-1970s belonged to either the International Socialists (later the Socialist Workers Party), or the supposedly more 'radical' International Marxist Group, the reigning two at the time. Both obviously purported to believe in much the same things: the former 'stood against all forms of exploitation, bigotry and oppression' in the belief that 'a socialist world where people came before profit [was] possible and necessary'; the latter sought the 'overthrow of imperialist capitalism followed by the setting up of a government based on direct democratic control by the people.'[2]

I thought it was all too theoretical, too far removed from real life, and not helped by some of the people spouting it. There were many for whom it was obviously the 'opiate of the people' that Karl Marx levelled against religion (but omitting, significantly enough, the second part of the quote, which is that it was also 'the heart of a heartless world'), with *Das Kapital* simply replacing the Bhagavad Gita, the Bible, Confucianism, the Kojiki, the Quran. Joni fell into this category, hence his disillusionment, unlike those for whom it was simply a matter of fashion, as I saw when I reconnected with one of the latter during a recent visit to Swansea in 2018 after so many years. He wasn't in the least disillusioned by the absence of a revolution but had happily settled for a Labour Party that was shortly to exorcise its 'radical' wing the better to support the Gaza genocide that was just beginning to unfold mere days into my present journey, the single greatest crime so far this century.

*

I am conscious that Nigeria has dominated this narrative, but it could hardly be otherwise given its sheer heft in the region, as I hope I have managed to convey. As I told Sherriff, my newfound friend in Guinea-Bissau who hosted me, my Surulere local government area in Lagos State—one of twenty altogether and by no means the most densely populated—contained one-third of his entire country's two million. That much is conceded, and yet no story of West Africa can be complete without mentioning the towering figure of Amílcar Cabral, who led the fight to free Portuguese Guinea (as it was then known, along with Cape Verde, the other country I didn't visit), from 1953 until he was assassinated in 1963, just one year before the country was granted independence. (The name of his killer is known to history but will not be mentioned here.) To at least one commentator, he was akin to Sékou Touré of Guinea-Conakry and Nelson Mandela of South Africa in their different ways; he was also lauded by Fidel Castro as 'one of the most lucid and brilliant leaders in Africa... who instilled in us tremendous confidence in the future and the success of his struggle for liberation.'[3]

And struggle he did. Unlike the British and French (and, indeed, the Spanish with their Equatorial Guinea's murderous dictator), the Portuguese military dictatorship was not prepared to let go of their colonies under any circumstances and duly put boots on the ground, here as well as in Angola and Mozambique. Cabral, who won a scholarship to study agronomy in Lisbon, began to show his political leanings when he helped found the Centro de Estudos Africanos, an association of Lusophone African students that included the future Angolan president, Agostinho Neto. After he graduated in 1950, he returned home and was employed by the colonial authorities in his chosen field, which enabled him to travel widely conducting a survey of the land and its resources, and to interact with people from various cultures roped together in the colony. In 1956, he and five associates—including a brother, Luís—formed the African Party for the Independence of Guinea and Cape Verde (Partido Africano da Independência da Guiné e Cabo Verde, PAIGC).

Cabral rapidly emerged as the leader of the PAIGC, which began by organising workers' strikes calling for better wages and improved conditions. However, the so-called Pidjiguiti Massacre in August 1959, when the Portuguese fired on demonstrators during a dockworkers' strike, demonstrated that a different approach was required, which was to shift to the countryside using guerrilla-style tactics. To that end, Cabral set up camps in Ghana with the blessing of Kwame Nkrumah. His lieutenants were trained to provide them with effective communication skills to aid their efforts in mobilising Guinean traditional leaders to support the PAIGC, but he also realised that the war effort could only be sustained if his troops could be fed and taught to live off the land, alongside the larger populace, who themselves could be taught better farming techniques to increase productivity. When not fighting, PAIGC soldiers tilled and ploughed the fields alongside the locals. PAIGC also set up a trade-and-barter bazaar system that moved around the country and made staple goods available to the countryside at prices lower than that of colonial-owned stores. During the war, Cabral established a roving hospital and triage station to give medical care to wounded

PAIGC soldiers and quality-of-life care to the larger populace, relying on medical supplies from the then USSR and Sweden.

By all accounts a modest man, he exhorted his comrades to always be open and honest as they went about their work:

> We must practice revolutionary democracy in every aspect of our Party life. Every responsible member must have the courage of his responsibilities, exacting from others a proper respect for his work and properly respecting the work of others. Hide nothing from the masses of our people. Tell no lies. Expose lies whenever they are told. Mask no difficulties, mistakes, failures. Claim no easy victories.[4]

He was also something of an idealist with his concept of 're-Africanisation', which was for the continent's necessarily minority elite, otherwise beholden to the colonisers for their education and employment, to rediscover their traditional cultures. This would enable them to reintegrate with the rural peasantry whose lives had remained largely untouched by imperialism. He called this 'Returning to the Source'. Alas, this same elite, in Bissau as elsewhere in the continent, has merely perpetuated its elitism as it continues to despise the masses who are mocked for their poor or non-existent English, French, Portuguese or Spanish, as the case may be.

As for Guinea-Bissau itself, Cabral would be mortified by what it has become, although whether he would have been able to do better had he lived—or been allowed to live—is a moot point. As many observers have pointed out, there was no state to inherit when Portugal abruptly pulled out following a left-wing military coup in Lisbon—the so-called 'Carnation Revolution'—that ousted the fascist junta and led the way for the independence of the colonial territories, but the foundations of the new state were fragile from the start:

> The destruction wrought by the liberation war meant there was no organised state on which to build. The victorious [PAIGC] was the

dominant political force, and internal party patronage networks quickly began to dominate those economic resources that were available. In a context of relative resource scarcity, and the failure to establish a working state, infighting within the ruling elite was intense; since independence no elected President has been able to complete his term in office. All but one were deposed by the military, and the exception, Nino Vieira, was assassinated by soldiers. The defining feature of politics in Guinea-Bissau has been conflict and chronic instability. Understanding what has driven that instability must centre on the coalescence of elite networks around economic interests. Since independence, the Bissau-Guinean elite has been constituted by a tight web of political, military and business figures who have reconstituted themselves 'in fluctuating and ambiguous alliances'. Their interests have centred around securing economic opportunity for themselves, as opposed to the state.[5]

The process of 'securing economic opportunity' was drugs. At the turn of the millennium, Guinea-Bissau was designated Africa's first 'narco-state' by the UN, helped in no small part by the clampdown in Jamaica and Panama, both former transit points for smuggling drugs into Europe, along with the extra scrutiny with which European governments handled parcels from South America. According to an official at the United States Drug Enforcement Administration:

> the logical thing is for cartels to take the shortest crossing over the ocean [from Colombia] to West Africa, by plane—to one of the many airstrips left behind by decades of war, or by drop into the thousands of little bays—or by boat all the way. A ship can drop anchor in waters completely unmonitored, while fleets of smaller craft take the contraband ashore.[6]

The boats themselves travel only at night; in the daytime, they are covered by blue tarpaulins to avoid detection from the air, and only made possible by the direct involvement of the military, as was blown open in 2013 with the arrest in the US of José

Américo Bubo Na Tchuto, ex-head of the navy, who was caught on a luxury yacht as he was closing a deal that would have netted him US$1m for a tonne of cocaine transited through the country. He served his time. According to a local restaurant owner, 'this country is being destroyed by drugs. They're everywhere. A few weeks ago, the man who used to be my gardener knocked at the door and offered to sell me [approximately 15 pounds] of cocaine.'[7] My host, a young man I met the day I arrived who gave over to me his self-contained bedroom while he managed the narrow passageway, certainly agreed with that assessment. His own mother was an addict.

*

So, there we have it. Guinea-Bissau, the ECOWAS country with the lowest number of inhabitants, and Nigeria, with the most by a factor of a hundred, both narco-states, the one a transit point, the other ruled by a drug baron. They are also conjoined by the fact—in common with all the others—that they are artificial creations of foreign conquering powers with their own agendas. Even the British, understanding first-hand the complexity of their own creation, and imagining they were going to rule for a hundred years, apparently made provision in the original 1914 amalgamation for the entity to cease to exist after a century if the people so chose. Or so I understand. I once attempted to track down the relevant document but was turned away when I visited the UK National Archives some years ago.

On the other hand, the chances are there may not be a Nigeria for very much longer. The disintegration is happening as I write, and will probably be sealed in 2027, when the next national elections are due even as the current upstart plots his re-election with no concern for why he wants power but for its own sake, having made more people poorer in just his first two years. According to the latest Unicef report, around 11 million children under the age of five, which is to say one in every three, are experiencing severe child food poverty, making them up to fifty per cent more likely to experience wasting, a life-threatening form of malnutrition. This is unsustainable, as we are discovering.

The break-up of Nigeria into smaller, more coherent units is inevitable. On the surface, this will also mean yet more useless seats in the 'who and who unite for United Nations', as Fẹlá Kúti succinctly put it. With seventeen per cent of the world's population, Africa already has 54 of the 193 members but without a single permanent seat on the Security Council. To that end, Linda Thomas-Greenfield, the African American immediate past US representative, proudly announced in 2024 that two (unspecified) African countries would be considered for two permanent seats in the hallowed council in order that the continent might 'deliver the full benefit of their knowledge and voices', and added: 'It's what our African partners seek, and it's what we believe is just.'[8] However, this would come without the power of veto, which would make the council 'dysfunctional'. As currently obtains, this could only mean a choice between Egypt, Nigeria and South Africa, the three heavyweights by quite a distance, although the first of them is only African by geography and more properly belongs to the Arabic-speaking Middle East (along with the other countries in North Africa), which is why, all things being equal, the choice will narrow down to the other two.

All well and good, but the continent itself has long argued for this and more, notably at the African Union's fifth ordinary session held in Sirte, Libya twenty years ago, where it adopted the Ezulwini Consensus that envisaged 'not less than two permanent seats with all the prerogatives and privileges of permanent membership including the right of veto', along with five non-permanent seats, although it seems self-evident that the continent south of the Sahara should come together as one and insist on a permanent seat with full veto powers or withdraw from the organisation altogether, in keeping with Kwame Nkrumah's call more than six decades ago for 'a Union or Commonwealth of African States' that would 'achieve the complete liquidation of imperialism, colonialism and neocolonialism in Africa'. Offering the prospect of just two without the power of veto only seeks to maintain the intolerably patronising view of the continent, which is presumably why the then President Joe Biden chose a descendant of the enslaved to utter the insult. But then this was the same woman who used her country's veto to uphold the ongoing genocide in Gaza in favour of 'Israel's right of self-defence,' while also ruling out the possibility of the Palestinian Authority to become a full UN member that would help towards a two-state solution to the seemingly intractable conflict: 'We do not see that doing a resolution in the Security Council will necessarily get us to a place where we can find...a two-state solution moving forward.'

Even more patronising was the address of her deputy, Robert Wood, to the same UN, where he admonished the Palestinian Authority 'to undertake necessary reforms to help establish the attributes of readiness for statehood', while noting that Hamas, 'a terrorist organization...is currently exerting power and influence in Gaza, an integral part of the state envisioned in this resolution.' In his country's view, 'the most expeditious path toward statehood for the Palestinian people is through direct negotiations between Israel and the Palestinian Authority with the support of the United States and other partners.'[9] Listening to these two, you wouldn't have imagined that 'the history of Palestine', as detailed by Haris Rahim in *The Thought Archive* (October 2023), 'is marked by a rich tapestry of civilizations, conflicts, and cultural developments, spanning thousands of years

EPILOGUE

from ancient times to the present day' until the 1948 settlement to assuage the European conscience, but slave is a slave is a slave, as in the case of Michael Langley.

Langley is the first African American four-star general in the US Marine Corps. He also happens to be the current commander of the US Africa Command, which, 'with partners, counters transnational threats and malign actors, strengthens security forces and responds to crises in order to advance U.S. national interests and promote regional security, stability and prosperity.' According to Langley's testimony before the US senate, Traoré (presumably one of the perceived 'malign actors') was using his country's gold to secure himself and his family: 'Absolutely, Chairman. I see this, and I don't mind calling it out. Captain [Ibrahim] Traoré in Burkina Faso... their gold reserves are just in exchange to protect the junta regime.'[10] For Traoré himself, the fact that it was a black man who said this was what 'hurt me the most' and he hoped that he would 'look at himself in the mirror, feel ashamed, come out and say...I regret it': 'If he was sent...to understand that this was not the right mission. If he was misled, he should say so publicly... If it was done with bad intentions, well, we will confront him as we should. Because everything he said is a lie, and it's really shameful to see an adult lie.'[11]

At first the general resisted, doubling down on his statement: 'It is an insult asking me to apologize to Ibrahim. I am a four-star General of the United States Marines protecting the interests of the American government. He is brain-washing the African people and he has to stop.'[12] But this 'Uncle Tom in uniform', hoping to please Massa, had underestimated the outcry across the continent (including a video 'from his roots in Senegal' telling him that he had dishonoured himself on the grounds that 'one does not fight his brother'), whereupon he capitulated, presumably on Massa's orders:

I made a mistake. I let my position cloud my judgment. Captain Ibrahim Traoré is not stealing gold; he is reclaiming what belongs to his people. I was wrong, and I apologize. This is personal to me because I am African. My roots are African. In my desire to please the wrong people, I forgot that. I forgot what it means to fight for freedom. Captain Traoré, if you're watching this, I'm sorry. I spoke out of ignorance and pressure, not truth.[13]

Traoré's response only raised him higher in the eyes of the continent's teeming youth, 'we accept your apology not because we are weak but because we are strong enough to heal. Let your apology be the beginning of great things. We are not your enemies or inferiors but your equals.'[14] And then it turned out that Langley was allegedly part of an attempted coup in which arms from France would be shipped through Côte d'Ivoire, where they would be used by dissidents protected by Ouattara, as he continues to protect the man who killed Thomas Sankara. Ouattara, for his part, has never hidden his dislike of Traoré under the guise of disapproving military juntas, and who appears to have now paid the price.

*

On 19 May 2025, social media was ablaze with claims a coup was underway in Côte d'Ivoire. Various Facebook and X accounts posted videos of burning buildings, and of crowds and soldiers on the streets, all supposedly in Abidjan. Meanwhile, YouTube channels such as 'Ibrahim Traore Wife' uploaded video reports, some clearly AI-generated, alleging that Outtara had been overthrown. But all of this was a fantasy, and didn't, in fact, happen. One of the YouTube videos, 'They Captured Ouattara... Then Made Him Do the Unthinkable', itself stated that its stories were 'entirely fictional and created solely for entertainment purposes', but there were rumours of a coup for a full week

EPILOGUE

afterwards. In one, Ouattara had fled to Paris in the wee hours; in another, he was alive but in custody; in a third, he was dead. Those I spoke with in the country—and which put paid to the rumour that the internet had been shut down—were themselves confused, but what is certain is that elections are approaching in which Ouattara has the 'right' to stand for a fourth term, having 'reset' the constitution at the tail end of his otherwise second and final term as determined by the very constitution he had otherwise sworn to protect. He has not himself indicated whether he will do so, perhaps weighing up his options as an entitled, manipulative 'elder' who is hostage to the IMF; the 'teeming' youths, meanwhile, are entranced by the charismatic young Traoré, the only visible symbol of their possible future in the otherwise bleak landscape those same elders refuse to take responsibility for. Shine your eye; change don' come.

NOTES

1. 'Book of A Lifetime: The Viceroy of Ouidah, by Bruce Chatwin,' *Independent*, 8 August 2008.
2. W.E.B. Du Bois, 'Strivings of the Negro People', *Atlantic Monthly*, August 1897, https://www.theatlantic.com/magazine/archive/1897/08/strivings-of-the-negro-people/305446/
3. 'A new home for the African diaspora in Ghana stirs tensions,' NPR, 25 February 2024.
4. Rita Marley with Hetti Jones, *No Woman, No Cry: My Life with Bob Marley* (Pan, 2004).
5. David Browne, '"They Wanted Her to Shut Up and Be a Widow": How Rita Marley Overcame Tragedy and Revived the Family Brand', *Rolling Stone*, 23 July 2021, https://www.rollingstone.com/music/music-features/rita-marley-bob-marley-marley-family-1196913/
6. Ta Nehisi-Coates, *The Message* (Hamish Hamilton, 2025).
7. Aamna Mohdin, 'Equalities minister under fire for writing she does not "care about colonialism"', *Guardian*, 23 September 2021, https://www.theguardian.com/politics/2021/sep/23/kemi-badenoch-equalities-minister-reportedly-wrote-i-dont-care-about-colonialism
8. Kemi Badenoch, 16 January 2025, https://www.conservatives.com/news/kemi-rebuilding-trust-speech

9. Nigel Biggar, 'Kemi Badenoch is right about colonialism', *The Spectator*, 22 September 2021, https://www.spectator.co.uk/article/kemi-badenoch-is-right-about-colonialism/
10. See 'Nigeria: Kidney-plot politician Ike Ekweremadu jailed', BBC News, 5 May 2023, https://www.bbc.co.uk/news/uk-england-london-65494027
11. Timothy Enietan-Matthews, 'Ekweremadu's wife, Beatrice, returns to Nigeria after release from UK prison', RipplesNigeria, 22 January 2025, https://www.ripplesnigeria.com/ekweremadus-wife-beatrice-returns-to-nigeria-after-release-from-uk-prison/
12. Abdulqudus Ogundapo, 'Nigerian senator says N14 million monthly salary not enough to run office', *Premium Times*, 18 October 2024, https://www.premiumtimesng.com/news/746406-nigerian-senator-says-n14-million-monthly-salary-not-enough-to-run-office.html
13. Oladipọ Yemitan, *Madame Tinubu: Merchant and King-maker* (Ibadan: University Press, 1987).

2. FAR FROM MY FATHER

1. Spotlight Initiative, '16 facts about violence against women and girls in Nigeria,' Unicef.org, 25 November 2022., https://www.unicef.org/nigeria/reports/16-facts-about-violence-against-women-and-girls-nigeria
2. 'IWD: Pain of Widows in Nigeria and CBA Foundation's Drive To Assuage Them,' *The Nigerian Voice*, 23 June 2021.
3. 'How we narrowly escaped death from violent husbands—Survivors,' *Punch*, 4 December 2023.
4. 'I saw hell for killing abusive husband,' *9News Nigeria*, 8 July 2022.
5. Véronique Tadjo, *Far from My Father* (University of Virginia Press, 2014).
6. V.S. Naipaul, 'The Crocodiles of Yamoussoukro', *The New Yorker*, 6 May 1984, https://www.newyorker.com/magazine/1984/05/14/the-crocodiles-of-yamoussoukro

3. A CULTURE OF SILENCE

1. Kwame Nkrumah, *Africa Must Unite* (New York: Frederick A. Praeger, 1963).
2. Kabral Blay-Amihere, 'Press and Government in Africa', *Index on Censorship*, July 1987, https://journals.sagepub.com/doi/pdf/10.1177/030642208701600711
3. Flt. Lt. Jerry John Rawlings, *People's Daily Graphic*, 6 March 1989; quoted in Adéwálé Májà-Pearce, 'The Press in West Africa,' *Index on Censorship*, June/July 1990, Vol. 19, No. 6, p. 67.
4. Kabral Blay-Amihere, 'Ghana's Free Press', *Index on Censorship*, January 1987.
5. Adéwálé Májà-Pearce, 'Who's afraid of Wole Soyinka?', *Index on Censorship*, July 1988, https://journals.sagepub.com/doi/pdf/10.1080/03064228808534484
6. Ibid.
7. Ibid.
8. Catherine Ross, 'Americo-Liberians,' *Black Past*, 16 June 2009.
9. See Jonathan Ort, 'What Princeton Owes to Firestone's Exploitation of Liberia', Department of African American Studies, Princeton University, 13 December 2022, https://aas.princeton.edu/news/what-princeton-owes-firestones-exploitation-liberia
10. Ibid.
11. See Tim Naftali, 'Ronald Reagan's Long-Hidden Racist Conversation With Richard Nixon', *The Atlantic*, 30 July 2019, https://www.theatlantic.com/ideas/archive/2019/07/ronald-reagans-racist-conversation-richard-nixon/595102/
12. Adéwálé Májà-Pearce, 'The Press in West Africa,' *Index on Censorship*, June/July 1990, Vol. 19, No. 6, p. 60.
13. Adéwálé Májà-Pearce, 'Who's afraid of Wole Soyinka?'
14. Itemised below in the order of the countries I travelled through: Nigeria: crude oil, natural gas, coal, tin and columbite (which are the most economically valuable), but also gypsum, kaolin,

barite, gold, sapphires, topazes, aquamarines and uranium; Benin: crude oil, limestone and marble; Togo: phosphates, limestone, gold, diamonds, iron ore, gypsum, bauxite, manganese, zinc, rutile and marble; Ghana: crude oil, natural gas, gold, diamonds, manganese, bauxite, limestone and iron ore; Côte d'Ivoire: crude oil, natural gas, gold, diamonds, iron ore, bauxite and manganese; Liberia: gold, diamonds and iron ore; Sierra Leone: chromite, rutile, bauxite, columbite, gold and platinum, along with the ubiquitous diamonds; Guinea-Conakry: gold, diamonds, uranium, iron ore and bauxite (of which it holds almost half the world's total reserves); Guinea-Bissau: gold, diamonds, bauxite, phosphate rocks, graphite, limestone and clay; The Gambia: zircon, titanium, laterite, clay and silica; Senegal: crude oil, natural gas, gold, aluminium, iron ore and phosphates; Mali: gold, uranium, diamonds, copper, iron ore, precious stones, zinc, manganese, bauxite, lead, lithium, bitumen schist, marble, gypsum, kaolin, phosphate, lignite, diatomic and rock salt; Burkina Faso: gold (the fourth largest reserves in the continent), copper, manganese, phosphate and limestone; and, finally, Niger: crude oil, gold, uranium (some of the world's largest reserves), coal, iron ore and tin.

4. THE STOLEN PEOPLE

1. That is, declared him dead. Alex Haley, *Roots: The Saga of an American Family – 30th Anniversary Edition* (Vanguard Press, 2007).
2. Esther Onyegbula, 'Police arrest couple for child abuse in Lagos,' *The Vanguard*, 2 June 2020.
3. 'Nigerian woman speaks of slavery and rape in UK', BBC News, 14 March 2024, https://www.bbc.co.uk/news/uk-england-cambridgeshire-68341674
4. Samantha Churchill, 'Carter Jackson's new book analyzes the

praises and criticisms of "Roots" and their relation to today's political climate,' *The Wellesley News*, 30 October 2017.
5. Alex Beam, 'The Prize Fight Over Alex Haley's Tangled "Roots"', *Boston Globe*, 30 October 1998.
6. Rachel Jones, 'The warriors of this West African kingdom were formidable—and female', *National Geographic*, 14 September 2022, https://www.nationalgeographic.com/history/article/the-true-story-of-the-women-warriors-of-dahomey

5. THE ARMY THAT TRUMPETS THE DEMOCRATIC CALL

1. SaharaTV, YouTube, 6 March 2018, https://www.youtube.com/watch?v=t5oU797Yp68.
2. Mersiha Gadzo, '"No justification for Gaza carnage": Nigeria Foreign Minister Yusuf Tuggar', Al Jazeera, 5 March 2024, https://www.aljazeera.com/features/2024/3/5/no-justification-for-gaza-carnage-nigeria-foreign-minister-yusuf-tuggar
3. Adéwálé Májà-Pearce, 'Once more unto the polls…', *Index on Censorship*, March 1996, https://journals.sagepub.com/doi/pdf/10.1080/03064229608536104
4. Ibid.

6. THE MOST SAVAGE ACTS

1. See Adéwálé Májà-Pearce, 'Feed the Charm', *London Review of Books*, 25 July 2002, https://www.lrb.co.uk/the-paper/v24/n14/adewale-maja-pearce/feed-the-charm
2. See 'Justice for Liberia: The Truth and Reconciliation Commission's Recommendation for an Internationalized Domestic War Crimes Court, December 2009', Human Rights Watch, https://www.hrw.org/sites/default/files/related_material/liberia1209_0.pdf
3. 'Did Ellen Johnson Sirleaf do enough for Liberia?', Al

Jazeera, 24 May 2019, https://www.aljazeera.com/video/upfront/2019/5/24/did-ellen-johnson-sirleaf-do-enough-for-liberia
4. Ibid.
5. 'Ellen Johnson Sirleaf wins 2017 Ibrahim Prize for Achievement in African Leadership', Ibrahim Foundation, 12 February 2018, https://mo.ibrahim.foundation/news/2018/ellen-johnson-sirleaf-wins-2017-ibrahim-prize-achievement-african-leadership
6. https://www.trcofliberia.org/resources/reports/final/trc-of-liberia-final-report-volume-ii.pdf
7. Marco Margaritoff, 'How General Butt Naked Went from a Ruthless Liberian Warlord to a Repentant Preacher', allthatsinteresting.com/general-butt-naked; 'In Liberia, General "Butt Naked" rehabilitates ex-child soldiers,' *Africa Insider*; 'Hired Killer Now Bares Only His Soul Liberian Fighter, Who Fought Without Clothes, Becomes Evangelical Preacher,' *The Spokesman-Review*, 4 August 1997.
8. Damon Tabor, 'The Greater the Sinner', *New Yorker*, 6 March 2016, https://www.newyorker.com/magazine/2016/03/14/general-butt-naked-the-repentant-warlord
9. See Tamasin Ford and Rachel Stevenson, 'Charles Taylor verdict: "He should taste the bitterness of the law"', *Guardian*, 24 April 2012, https://www.theguardian.com/world/2012/apr/24/charles-taylor-war-crimes-verdict
10. https://www.sierraleonetrc.org/index.php/view-the-final-report/download-table-of-contents

7. THE COLONISATION CONTINUATION PACT

1. Margery Perham, *Lugard: The Years of Authority: 1898–1945* (London: Collins, 1960).
2. Francois Mitterand, *Politique Française et Abandon* (1958).
3. Tony Chafer, 'Decolonization in French West Africa', Oxford Research Encyclopedias, 26 October 2017, https://

oxfordre.com/africanhistory/display/10.1093/acrefore/9780190277734.001.0001/acrefore-9780190277734-e-166

4. Adéwálé Májà-Pearce, 'Prospects for Ambazonia', *London Review of Books*, 25 October 2018, https://www.lrb.co.uk/the-paper/v40/n20/adewale-maja-pearce/prospects-for-ambazonia
5. Ibid.
6. Emmanuel Freudenthal, Frank William Batchou, and Gaelle Tjat, 'Paul Biya, Cameroon's Roaming President', OCCRP, 18 February 2018, https://www.occrp.org/en/investigation/paul-biya-cameroons-roaming-president
7. Pierre Nandjui, *Houphouët-Boigny: L'homme de la France en Afrique* (Paris: Harmattan, 1995).
8. John Reed and Clive Wake (eds), *L.S. Senghor: Prose and Poetry* (OUP, 1964), pp. 94–95.
9. Léopold Sédar Senghor, *Selected Poems* (London: Oxford University Press, 1964).

8. PLEASE, I'M BEGGING YOU

1. Adéwálé Májà-Pearce, 'Disabled Africa: rights not welfare', *Index on Censorship*, January 1998, https://journals.sagepub.com/doi/pdf/10.1080/03064229808536308
2. Ibid.
3. Ibid.
4. V.S. Naipaul, *Finding the Center: Two Narratives* (Knopf, 1984), p. 112.
5. 'Ivory Coast election: Alassane Ouattara wins amid boycott', BBC News, 3 November 2020, https://www.bbc.co.uk/news/world-africa-54778200
6. Baudelaire Mieu, 'Côte d'Ivoire: Ouattara reins in his troops at an emergency meeting', *The Africa Report*, 16 November 2020, https://www.theafricareport.com/50732/cote-divoire-ouattara-reins-in-his-troops-at-an-emergency-meeting/
7. Ibid.
8. From 'Africa: An Agenda for the Twenty-First Century',

International Monetary Fund, 23 September 1999, https://www.elibrary.imf.org/display/book/9781557758477/ch02.xml
9. 'Côte d'Ivoire: Post-Election Violence, Repression', Human Rights Watch, 2 December 2020, https://www.hrw.org/news/2020/12/02/cote-divoire-post-election-violence-repression
10. Antonio Cascais, 'Is the AU failing in its role as a mediator?', DW.com, 25 May 2023, https://www.dw.com/en/is-the-african-union-at-risk-of-failing-in-its-role-as-a-mediator/a-65730521
11. Neil Munshi, 'Ivory Coast's Alassane Ouattara secures third term in disputed poll', *Financial Times*, 3 November 2020, https://www.ft.com/content/af645e4b-658e-4254-be88-c377792be6e0
12. Benjamin Roger, Marwane Ben Yahmed, 'President Macron: "Between France and Africa, it must be a love story"', *The Africa Report*, 20 November 2020, https://www.theafricareport.com/51475/president-macron-between-france-and-africa-it-must-be-a-love-story/
13. See 'France is set to end the use of the 75-year-old controversial CFA franc in West Africa', CNN, 23 December 2019, https://edition.cnn.com/2019/12/23/africa/france-stops-use-of-cfa
14. 'Buhari and Ouattara make Eco heart of regional power struggle', *The Africa Report*, 12 February 2020, https://www.theafricareport.com/23374/buhari-and-ouattara-make-eco-heart-of-regional-power-struggle/
15. 'President Buhari Urges Caution on ECOWAS Common Currency', 23 June 2020, https://statehouse.gov.ng/news/president-buhari-urges-caution-on-ecowas-common-currency/

9. DO OR DIE

1. Adéwálé Májà-Pearce, 'Where to begin?', *London Review of*

NOTES

    Books, 26 April 2018, https://www.lrb.co.uk/the-paper/v40/n08/adewale-maja-pearce/where-to-begin
2. Ibid.
3. 'Baobab—The Upside Down Tree', SafarisAfricana.com.
4. Lindsey Jean Schueman, 'African baobab tree: how one plant creates an entire habitat', One Earth, 30 May 2024, https://www.oneearth.org/species-of-the-week-african-baobab-tree/
5. Matthew Daly, Seth Borenstein, 'Trump signs executive order directing US withdrawal from the Paris climate agreement—again', AP News, 21 January 2025, https://apnews.com/article/trump-paris-agreement-climate-change-788907bb89fe307a964be757313cdfb0
6. Damian Carrington, 'Climate change target of 2C is "dead", says renowned climate scientist', *Guardian*, 4 February 2025, https://www.theguardian.com/environment/2025/feb/04/climate-change-target-of-2c-is-dead-says-renowned-climate-scientist

10. A NATION IS NOT BUILT ON INDISCIPLINE AND DISORDER

1. 'Mali names coup leader Col Assimi Goïta as transitional president', BBC News, 29 May 2021, https://www.bbc.co.uk/news/world-africa-57290761
2. Rahmane Idrissa, 'In Bamako', *London Review of Books*, 2 February 2023, https://www.lrb.co.uk/the-paper/v45/n03/rahmane-idrissa/diary
3. 'Niger general Tchiani named head of transitional government after coup', Al Jazeera, 28 July 2023, https://www.aljazeera.com/news/2023/7/28/niger-general-tchiani-named-head-of-transitional-government-after-coup
4. 'Burkina Faso unrest: Military officers remove leader Damiba', BBC News, 1 October 2022, https://www.bbc.co.uk/news/world-africa-63098217

5. Alexandra Reza, 'Sankara and Mitterrand', *London Review of Books*, 4 December 2014, https://www.lrb.co.uk/the-paper/v36/n23/alexandra-reza/short-cuts
6. Ibid.
7. 'Thomas Sankara's speech at the United Nations General Assembly,' nofi, 4 October 2024.
8. 'Burkina Faso Prime Minister's Speech 44/19 Speech in Nicaragua', kawsachunnews.com, 21 July 2023, https://kawsachunnews.com/burkina-faso-prime-ministers-44-19-speech-in-nicaragua
9. 'Burkina Faso junta leader seeks Russia's nuclear energy support', TRT Global, 29 July 2023, https://trt.global/afrika-english/article/14249758
10. Post on X.com by @GoitaAssimi, 4 October 2022.
11. Tim Rogers, 'The Unraveling of Nicaragua', *The Atlantic*, 6 June 2018, https://www.theatlantic.com/international/archive/2018/06/nicaragua-ortega-protests/562094/
12. Ibid.
13. Karim Hauser, 'Nicaragua e Irán, "unión invincible"', BBC World Service (in Spanish), 11 June 2007. Archived from the original on 11 July 2012. Retrieved 9 March 2019.
14. Eli Alfred, 'Thomas Sankara's Bold Stand Against Food Aid: A Vision for Burkina Faso's Self-Sufficiency,' Cbgist News, 24 April 2025.
15. Steve Biko Wafula, 'In Two Years of President Ibrahim Traoré: The Renaissance of Burkina Faso and the Dawn of an African Awakening,' Soko Directory, 19 January 2025.
16. Elie Kabora, 'Mining sector: A gold refinery in 11 months' time in Ouagadougou,' Samao, 23 November 2023.
17. Jake Clifford, 'Africa Can Survive Without Relying on Loans from IMF And World Bank—Burkina Faso President,' NewsweekNG, 9 January 2025.
18. 'Mali, Niger and Burkina Faso establish Sahel security alliance', Al Jazeera, 16 September 2023, https://www.aljazeera.com/

NOTES

news/2023/9/16/mali-niger-and-burkina-faso-establish-sahel-security-alliance

19. 'Niger Republic: At 2nd ECOWAS Extraordinary Summit, President Tinubu Champions Dialogue to Resolve Impasse', 10 August 2023, https://statehouse.gov.ng/news/niger-republic-at-2nd-ecowas-extraordinary-summit-president-tinubu-champions-dialogue-to-resolve-impasse/
20. *Niger Food Security Brief,* USAID, May 2014, https://www.scribd.com/document/706413854/Niger-Food-Security-Brief-Final
21. Chinedu Okafor, 'Burkina Faso leader warns Tinubu and ECOWAS that they are prepared to fight', *Business Insider Africa,* 20 February 2024, https://africa.businessinsider.com/local/lifestyle/burkina-faso-leader-warns-tinubu-and-ecowas-that-they-are-prepared-to-fight/ewydnlt
22. '"No Soldiers, No Logistics, No Compassion": Burkina's Traoré on Reasons for Ecowas Withdrawal,' SPUTNIK Africa, 31 January 2024.
23. Ibid.
24. Hugh Schofield, 'Macron looks on as France's Africa policy crumbles', BBC News, 2 September 2023, https://www.bbc.co.uk/news/world-europe-66668094
25. Adam Nossiter, 'Chad Strongman Says Nigeria Is Absent in Fight Against Boko Haram', *New York Times,* 27 March 2015, https://www.nytimes.com/2015/03/28/world/africa/chad-strongman-says-nigeria-is-absent-in-fight-against-boko-haram.html
26. Adéwálé Májà-Pearce, 'Where to begin?'
27. Debora Patta, Sarah Carter, 'Russia's Wagner Group accused of using rape and mass-murder to control an African gold mining town', CBS News, 25 May 2023, https://www.cbsnews.com/news/russia-wagner-group-central-african-republic-bambari-massacre-rape-mass-murder/
28. Jennifer Hauser and Tara John, 'Wagner boss Yevgeny Prigozhin

claims to be making Africa "freer" in unverified video', CNN, 21 August 2023, https://edition.cnn.com/2023/08/21/europe/russia-yevgeny-prigozhin-africa-desert-intl/index.html
29. Colin P. Clarke, 'If Your Country Is Falling Apart, the Wagner Group Will Be There', *New York Times*, 11 August 2023, https://www.nytimes.com/2023/08/11/opinion/wagner-russia-prigozhin-bazoum-niger.html
30. 'Burkina Faso: Traoré admits forcibly conscripting an editor as journalist kidnappings rise', RSF, 12 July 2024, https://rsf.org/en/burkina-faso-traor%C3%A9-admits-forcibly-conscripting-editor-journalist-kidnappings-rise
31. Khadidiatou Cissé, 'Burkina Faso outcry over "conscription used to punish junta critics"', BBC News, 7 February 2024, https://www.bbc.co.uk/news/world-africa-68166717
32. Ibid.
33. Samuel Fury Childs Daly, *Soldier's Paradise: Militarism in Africa after Empire* (Durham, NC: Duke University Press, 2024).

EPILOGUE

1. 'Nigeria's illegal refiners take quality edge', Energy Voice, 21 May 2020, https://www.energyvoice.com/oilandgas/africa/241148/nigerias-illegal-refiners-take-quality-edge/
2. See https://socialistworker.co.uk/join-swp/; and https://archives.lse.ac.uk/records/INTERNATIONAL_MARXIST_GROUP
3. Victoria Brittain, 'Africa: a continent drenched in the blood of revolutionary heroes', *Guardian*, 17 January 2011, https://www.theguardian.com/global-development/poverty-matters/2011/jan/17/lumumba-50th-anniversary-african-leaders-assassinations
4. Amilcar Cabral, *Revolution in Guinea, stage 1* (London, 1974), p. 72 (translated by Richard Handyside).
5. *Journal of Modern African Studies*, Vol. 53, No. 3 (2015), pp. 339–364 (Cambridge University Press, 2015).

NOTES

6. Ed Vulliamy, 'How a tiny West African country became the world's first narco state', *Guardian*, 9 March 2008, https://www.theguardian.com/world/2008/mar/09/drugstrade
7. Vulliamy, 'How a tiny West African country became the world's first narco state'.
8. Edith M. Lederer, 'US backs 2 permanent seats for African nations on the UN Security Council,' AP News, 13 September 2024.
9. 'Remarks at a UN General Assembly Debate on the U.S. Veto of a UN Security Council Resolution on Palestinian Membership', United States Mission to the United Nations, 1 May 2024, https://usun.usmission.gov/remarks-at-a-un-general-assembly-debate-on-the-u-s-veto-of-a-un-security-council-resolution-on-palestinian-membership/
10. Solomon Ekanem, 'South Africa's EFF rejects U.S. claims on Burkina Faso gold', *Business Insider Africa*, 21 April 2025, https://africa.businessinsider.com/local/lifestyle/south-africas-eff-rejects-us-claims-on-burkina-faso-gold/0s9t45m
11. https://www.youtube.com/watch?v=TaFcxv8qL1w.
12. 'US General Michael Langley Sparks Online Outrage', Ghana News, 14 May 2025, https://www.ghanamma.com/2025/05/14/us-general-michael-langley-sparks-online-outrage/
13. https://www.kingdomnubia.com/michel-langley-asks-captain-ibrahim-traore-for-forgiveness-for-his-comments-against-burkina-faso/
14. 'General Langley's Accusation Against Traoré: A Flashpoint in Africa's Struggle for Sovereignty', The Pan Afrikanist, 10 May 2025, https://thepanafrikanist.com/general-langleys-accusations-against-traore-a-flashpoint-in-africas-struggle-for-sovereignty/